The
Enjoyment

of
DRAMA

GOLDENTREE BOOKS

R. C. BALD, SAMUEL H. BEER & WILLIAM C. DEVANE
Series Editors

C. DAY LEWIS, Editor
English Lyric Poems, 1500–1900

DANIEL G. HOFFMAN and SAMUEL HYNES, Editors
English Literary Criticism (3 vols.): *The Renaissance;
Restoration and 18th Century; Romantic and Victorian*

KATHERINE LEVER
The Novel and the Reader

MILTON MARX
The Enjoyment of Drama, 2nd Edition

HAROLD OREL, Editor
The World of Victorian Humor

ROBERT L. PETERS, Editor
Victorians on Literature & Art

EDWARD STONE, Editor
Henry James: Seven Stories and Studies

MILTON MARX
University of Toledo

The

Enjoyment

of

DRAMA

Second Edition

New York
APPLETON-CENTURY-CROFTS, Inc.

PREFACE

THE MOST IMPORTANT CHANGES in the revised edition are the inclusion of new material on the conflict in drama, references to plays written and produced since the first edition, mention of television, which is an important factor in the story of drama today, and the omission of material that seems less important now than it did twenty years ago. Minor changes and revisions appear throughout the book. The principles of drama do not change much over the years, but the applications and illustrations of the principles may vary as conditions in the theater and in the world change.

The section on Dominative and Defensive Conflict first appeared in the *Quarterly Journal of Speech*. I wish to thank Elmer Rice for permission to quote from *The Adding Machine*, and Professor Joe Lee Davis, of the University of Michigan, who criticized the original manuscript and suggested many improvements. My special thanks are due to Arthur Miller, who has permitted me to quote from his critical writings and from *Death of a Salesman*.

I trust the book will retain its old friends and make new ones. Drama is meant to be enjoyed, and I hope this book will help to increase that enjoyment.

MILTON MARX

The University of Toledo

CONTENTS

Chapter 1

THE PURPOSE AND AIM OF DRAMA

OF ALL THE ARTS, drama is the closest to the people. No other art depends so much on the human element. The fullest enjoyment of a play comes from seeing it acted by a group of actors performing for another group, the audience. Every performance of a play is therefore different from every other performance, inasmuch as the actors never quite repeat themselves, and the audiences are continually changing. A single individual may, in solitude, read a play with pleasure and profit, and many plays are perhaps best enjoyed in this way; but the communal feeling between audience and actors is unquestionably one of the main reasons why the drama has always been popular.

The instinct for drama is universal in man. Children are born actors, and nothing delights them more than to play at pretending to be what they are not—their elders, their playmates, characters they have read or heard about in stories, or seen on television, even animals and supernatural beings. Their "play at pretending," to the great delight of themselves and their audience, is the root of all drama. When primitive man came home to his family, after several days' absence, bearing a slain animal on his shoulders, and told the story of his adventure, he revealed his ability as a narrator or perhaps even as a minstrel or a bard; when he acted out the story for the edification of his family and friends, as it is not unreasonable to suppose that he might have done, he presented possibly the first drama. It is easy to imagine his actions, first as himself, stalking his prey, then as the hunted animal at length brought down after a struggle, and finally as himself again, standing victorious over the body, beating his chest triumphantly with his fists to proclaim his own invincibility and the superiority of man over beast.

If the primitive actor, warming up to his audience, began to exaggerate some of the details of the story, making the animal more ferocious than he really was, the hunt more dangerous, and himself more heroic, he was only doing what most playwrights and actors have been doing ever since. And the primitive audience, shivering with apprehension over the risks their hero was running, although knowing all the while of his ultimate success, and sighing with relief at the final scene of victory, was revealing the characteristics of all future audiences. Man likes to show off before his fellows; audiences delight in experiencing, vicariously, the adventures of others.

The kinship of actors and audiences has existed from the beginning. Sometimes it has been very close, as when the actor's word or deed called forth a vociferous response from the audience. The actor in Shakespeare's time spoke from a platform stage that extended into the audience, who surrounded it on three sides, and to whom he often spoke directly and intimately, with immediate effect, as in the final speeches of *As You Like It* and *A Midsummer Night's Dream*. The "Vice" in the old morality plays often ran through the audience chasing his victim, to the accompaniment of encouraging or disparaging shouts. In the *Commedia dell' arte* of the Italian theater, the actors, playing stated roles in a standard repertoire of plays, were trained to improvise their lines, adapting them to the moods of the audience. No parts were written out as they are today, yet the actors were said to work together most skillfully, giving smooth, highly polished performances.

Audiences have always expressed their appreciation of the drama openly and directly. Applause and cheers as a sign of approval, boos and hisses as a mark of disapproval, are a natural part of the performance and the greatest possible compliment to the performers. The "play at pretending" has communicated itself from the stage to the audience, as it must do if the play is to be really successful, and even the theater itself seems to have been transformed into part of a room, or a king's palace, or Illyria. The perfect fusion of all three —actors, audience, and theater—is the recurring miracle that the actor anxiously awaits at every performance, for its absence tells him that the play is not "going over," as its occurrence assures him that the play is "made." And the applause and boos are not interruptions; they are spontaneous outbursts of feeling from audiences in tune with the actors.

We all like to pretend, but unlike children, most of us usually prefer to be by ourselves when we do so. Man comes nearest to achieving his potentialities in daydreams, when his imagination takes him wherever he wishes to go and makes him whatever he wishes to be. Daydreaming is not only a means of escape from the realities of everyday living, but indulges to the full man's desire for pretending. The secret life of Walter Mitty is the secret life of much of mankind. In the theater, man can daydream and pretend in the company of others. The spell a great actor or a great play casts on an audience is a most impressive example of mass daydreaming and pretending.

What the audience watches and listens to in such a performance is the art of the playwright, to which is added the art of the actor. The playwright conceives the story, the characters, and the dialogue; the actor brings them to life. The interest of the audience is thus a double one—in the story itself as it is unfolded on the stage, and in the way it is presented. And the pleasure the audience receives depends as much on the actor as it does on the playwright. Like music, drama gives the greatest pleasure when it is interpreted by a third person. There are those who can read music to themselves and enjoy hearing it only mentally; but music is meant to be played aloud—the fullest effects are gained in performance. As the musician is to the music, the actor is to the play. He gives it interpretation, but mainly he gives it life.

Some of the greatest stories in literature are in the dramatic form. *Hamlet, King Lear, Oedipus, Everyman, Cyrano de Bergerac,* to name but a few, are literary masterpieces in their own right, but unlike literary works written in other forms, they may at any time be brought to life as dramatic masterpieces. In fact, most of the great plays were written with a definite actor in mind (*Hamlet* and *King Lear* were written for Richard Burbage, an actor in Shakespeare's company; *Cyrano* was written to order for the French actor Coquelin.) They become a permanent part of literature after they have lived their natural life on the stage.

Reading a play, satisfactory though it may be to some, especially those with a vivid imagination, can never take the place of seeing it in a theater. The reader may have read and studied a play dozens of times, but until he has seen a capable company of actors perform it before an audience, the play has never really come to life for him. The great performers of the past still live in the recorded memoirs of those who saw and heard them—Mrs. Siddons, said to be the greatest English actress, as Lady Macbeth, David Garrick as King Lear, Edmund Kean in a number of Shakespearean roles. Several generations ago Sarah Bernhardt and Edwin Booth were vivid memories. Audiences of today treasure their memories of Laurence Olivier as Hamlet or Henry V, Julie Harris as Joan of Arc, Lee Cobb as Willy Loman; and in the realm of television, which is an important part of current drama, who can forget Maurice Evans as Macbeth, Mary Martin as Peter Pan, or Raymond Burr as Perry Mason? Seeing performances such as these are memorable experiences, more vividly recorded in the mind than is the reading of the plays from the printed page.

The significance of calling a drama a "play" or a "show" is often overlooked, but the two terms, like so many others in the vernacular, are most apt. The playwright (*play+maker*) makes the play, the actor acts it, the audience watches it. The element of play, of enjoyment, is uppermost in the minds of all three. Another element of drama, that of display, is illustrated by the expressions "the producer puts on the show," "a minor character steals the show," "the audience thought it was a good show." To put on a good show, either on or off the stage, means to make a good impression on those who are watching. Everyone concerned with the producing of a play—writer, director, actor, scene designer, and others, down to the stage hands—is primarily interested in putting on a good show and pleasing the audience. The drama appeals to the love of play and of display, and its devotees are both those who enjoy taking part and those who enjoy watching.

All art has a purpose. The artist does not work aimlessly, creating a work of art by accident. His purpose is usually the creation of beauty, by means of his own particular medium of expression, for the world in general to appreciate, if possible, or else for the few who can really understand what he is trying to do. *The purpose of drama is to entertain; the aim of drama is to tell a story.* Like other artists, the playwright is gratified by the applause of the multitude, and is glad when his play has given pleasure to many. But often he may not care to entertain the many; the story he has to tell may be meant for a select group, whose opinion, coming from those qualified to judge, he values more than the voice of general approval.

To entertain means much more than to amuse, for tragedy entertains as well as comedy. The moving story of King Lear or Everyman is better entertainment to many than the buffoonery of Falstaff or the wisecracks of Groucho Marx. The word *entertain* is derived from the Latin *tenere*, to hold. The holding of an audience in rapt attention, whether the play be grim tragedy, riotous farce, or quiet comedy, is the ambition of every actor; to be held in rapt attention, to forget everything save what is happening on the stage, is what the playgoer chiefly desires, is the real reason for his going to the theater. When the playgoer, at the end of the play he has just witnessed, is eager to leave the theater and get out into the fresh air, the entertainment has been superficial, little more than temporary amusement; but if he is reluctant to leave the theater, if he tries to prolong the spell cast by the play, to postpone his return to the world outside, the entertainment has become an experience he will treasure for a long time.

If the general purpose of drama is to entertain, its more specific aim is to tell a story. An audience may be held by a lecture or an oration, but the attention is not the same as that given a play. The illusion of being a part of what is happening on the stage is lacking, the audience being merely listeners, not participators. The telling of a tale "which holdeth children from play, and old men from the chimney corner," has always been the surest way of holding an audience, inside the theater or out. The enactment of a story by a group of actors is the special province of the drama.

But entertainment and storytelling are not the whole of drama. The important playwrights usually have some serious idea behind the entertainment, and the story, although it is meant first of all to be enjoyed, often contains food for thought on matters of interest to the individual or society. Not that the drama should preach a

sermon. "The playwright must never preach objectively," was the
wise dictum of James A. Herne, American playwright of the last
century, "but he should always teach subjectively." Artists have always had a message to give to the world—their urge to express
themselves in terms of their art is largely the result of their having
something to say coupled with the uncontrollable desire to say it.

The enjoyment of drama may take several forms. First, plays may
be enjoyed as literary masterpieces, comparable with other great
works of literature. The student of the classics studies the plays of
Aeschylus, Sophocles, and Euripides along with the epics of
Homer; and the plays of the Romans are to his mind an important
part of Latin literature. Shakespeare's plays are the glory of English
literature. The important modern plays are discussed in the same
breath as the significant novels of the day. This approach to the appreciation and evaluation of the drama makes use of Matthew
Arnold's "touchstone" method of criticism, the principle of the absolute standard, one so exacting that only a few works meet the requirements, the measure of worth being not whether or not the
work has met the test, but how close it has come to it. Such a severe
standard of judgment is helpful in criticizing a masterpiece, and is
perhaps the only way to arrive at a final evaluation, but it will not
guide the reader of drama consistently, since many a play worth
consideration may be far from being a world masterpiece, and yet
be a successful drama.*

A second point of view is the historical. The Greek plays represent a certain period in the development of dramatic art. Why
were they as they were when they were? Why did they come when
they did? Why did they die? The Roman drama, which succeeded
the Greek, was different in form and content. Medieval Europe en-
couraged the drama only as a function of the church. The Renaissance saw a widespread revival of secular drama. The plays of
Shakespeare and his contemporaries were expressive of all the
multifarious interests of their age. In fact, the term "Elizabethan
drama" has connotations peculiarly its own, as have the terms
"Restoration drama," "neoclassical drama," the "drama of sensi-

* See Chapter 9 on "How to Judge a Play."

bility," "closet drama" as applied to one phase of nineteenth-century playwriting, and "modern drama," (which is often used as synonymous with "contemporary drama" but is by some critics distinguished from it). Is there a connected story linking one age of drama with the next? Are there reasons for sudden outbursts of dramatic activity that are followed by periods of comparative quiet? In a survey of drama as a whole, from the Greek period to the present, is there discernible a development, a progression toward a definite goal, presumably not yet reached?

Part of the historical approach is the study of drama as a reflection of the life of the time in which it was written. The playwright often refers and alludes to everyday or recent happenings. It is a commonplace of criticism to say that Shakespeare's plays appealed to every one in his audiences. The number of contemporary allusions in the plays, especially in the comic lines, illustrates one method of holding the interest, and these same lines are of interest today just because they show us what interested audiences then.

When Hamlet gives his advice to the players, "Speak the speech, I pray you, as I pronounced it to you, trippingly on the tongue," the original audiences knew that they were listening to criticism of actors of the day, and we who hear the speech now know it too; in fact, we think that Shakespeare the actor-manager is perhaps here talking directly to his actors. When a little later Hamlet says, "And let those that play your clowns speak no more than is set down for them." we realize that Shakespeare is inveighing against the practice, which he abhorred, of adding lines to those the author had written, for no better purpose than to make the groundlings laugh. And when, previously in the play, Rosencrantz tells Hamlet of the coming of the players to Elsinore, and that they are not so prosperous as formerly, because "there is, sir, an aery of little children, little eyases, that cry out on the top of question, and are most tyrannically clapped for't," the reference is to the growing popularity of companies of child actors who were taking the bread out of the mouths of the professional actors. We are reading contemporary accounts of conditions of the times.

Comedies, especially satirical comedies, and burlesques tell much about the life of the times. Aristophanes pokes fun at Euripi-

des and the "New Tragedy" in *The Frogs;* the contest between
Euripides and Aeschylus is ludicrous; but if we can see through the
satire, we can probably get a truer conception of what the average
Greek thought of the serious playwrights of the time than we can in
any other way. The picture of Socrates and the "New Learning" in
The Clouds is obviously an exaggeration, but it is a contemporary
portrait from the point of view of the man in the street. One of the
best ways to understand the English heroic play of the Restoration
is through a study of the *The Rehearsal*, the burlesque by Bucking-
ham and others that satirized Dryden in particular as well as the
heroic plays in general. The careful student of this play will note
also parodies of seventeen specific heroic plays, the authors
apparently assuming a knowledge on the part of the audiences of
lines, passages, and characters. The play was thus addressed to a
special audience (the Restoration audiences were small, and the
same persons went to the theater again and again); and if we are
to enjoy the criticism too we must equip ourselves with its knowledge of details.

Contemporary satiric plays, which amuse and delight us because they attack the foibles, manners, customs, and institutions of
the day, will be an invaluable guide to the future critic looking for
material that will reveal something about our life. A play like
Destry Rides Again and the *Maverick* series on television reflect the
tendencies of our audiences to laugh at the artificialities and exaggerations of the popular Westerns of today. Sid Caesar has satirized
almost every type of theatrical entertainment, delighting his millions of viewers on television. At the same time, the critic will find,
audiences that welcomed such satire continued to patronize the
very type of play that had fun poked at it just as the audiences that
laughed at *The Rehearsal* in the seventeenth century continued to
go to see heroic plays. In other words, satire seems to be effective
for the moment, but human nature does not change very rapidly.

But it is not alone through direct references and allusions that
the drama reflects the life of the times. The plays of every age often
reveal the characteristic thought of the age as well as the individual
playwright's attitude on the subject about which he is writing. In
the Greek dramatic world the general assumption, even though it

may be questioned at times, is that the Fates rule human lives; the world created by Shakespeare is essentially a moral one, and although good often goes down to defeat, evil is always eventually punished; the background of Restoration drama is a frank, often cynically humorous, outlook on sex and marriage; the drama of the Age of Reason, both in France and England, has a kind of classical serenity; nineteenth century drama shows the awakening of both a humanitarian conscience and a revolutionary consciousness with reference to social injustice; the drama of the twentieth century shows an increasing interest in social welfare, the rights of the common man, the problem of living in a troubled world. Contemporary American drama seems preoccupied with the small details of everyday life of ordinary people; it is as though our playwrights today, in an age of atomic energy and outer space adventure, seek refuge in the commonplace.

A third point of view is what we may call the biographical. Although plays may be seen or read individually, each considered by itself, the whole body of a playwright's work may be thought of as a unit, each part of which reflects a phase of the writer's development as an artist or as a personality. Thus *Hamlet* and *King Lear* are Shakespeare's masterpieces; each is a great work of art; one may have read nothing else of Shakespeare and yet have some conception of the world's foremost playwright. If, however, one has read all the known plays of Shakespeare, in the order in which they were presumably written, he will become aware that *Hamlet* and *King Lear* are intimately connected as expressions of a definite period in their author's thought and feeling. The thirty-seven plays taken together form a structure, with a beginning, middle, and end, as artistically composed as though it had been designed. We know few of the external facts of Shakespeare's life, but through a study of his plays we can reconstruct the nature of his inner life, the mutations of his emotional and intellectual growth.

We may approach the plays of Ibsen biographically, and study his development as a craftsman and as a thinker. Many of the plays of Eugene O'Neill are autobiographical, in the sense that they were based on actual events in his life; the posthumous *Long Day's Journey Into Night* and *Touch of the Poet* are almost embarrass-

ingly personal. In a broad sense, of course, all literature is autobiographical. An author writes what and as he does because he is
what he is. The biographical approach to the drama (or to other
forms of literature) is most important. Academic courses that deal
with such writers as Shakespeare or Ibsen often use this approach
as a basis.

A fourth point of view is that of the director, whose business is
stage production. When he reads a play, his evaluation and judgment are quite different from those of the student or the general
reader. The director sees it mainly in terms of movement, rhythm,
color, and actors who can portray the roles. As he reads, he continually visualizes the scenes as they will appear in the finished
production. He plans where the actors will stand at any given moment, what gestures they will use, how they will read their lines. He
sees the background he wants for the actors, the lighting effects.
His whole concern is to bring the play to life in the theater.

The difference between O'Neill's *Ah, Wilderness!* as a stage play,
as a motion picture, and as a television play, was a matter of direction. The stage production was built around George M. Cohan,
who took the part of Nat Miller, the father in the early twentieth-
century household. The picture shifted the emphasis to Richard,
the adolescent son of the family. The television version was a combination of the two, about equal emphasis being placed on father
and son. The director, who transforms the manuscript of the playwright into the finished product, is a most important person in the
dramatic world today.

A fifth point of view is the technical or structural. The study of
the drama as an art form is especially interesting, and it is not
strange that of making many books on the theory and technique
of drama there is no end. The student and critic of the drama is
concerned with the ideas of the playwright and the story he has
to tell, but he is just as much concerned with the special form of
expression, the methods and devices used, the plan and structure
of the work. What principles of technique and structure are special
to the drama? Wherein is the difference between the dramatic
form and other literary forms? What are the problems of the play-

wright, and how may we best understand them, so that we will the more appreciate his work?

Finally, as a sort of common denominator, is the point of view of the audience that has come to the theater to "see the show." Whether its interest is literary, historical, biographical, technical, or more elemental, the audience desires to enjoy the spell cast by a theatrical performance on almost everyone present, before or behind the curtain. The attraction may be a famous actor, a famous producer or director, a famous play or playwright; it may be none of these, but merely the prospect of a pleasant way of passing the time; or it may be the appeal of the world of make-believe for those eager to escape, for the time being, the commonplaces of everyday life. The real lover of the theater enjoys everything the stage has to offer. If the play is bad, the acting may be good; if both are bad, something else will engross his attention. Serious drama may give him the most aesthetic satisfaction, but he gets as much pleasure from a good musical comedy. He sees nothing incongruous in giving full approval to Gilbert and Sullivan or Rodgers and Hammerstein in their *genre*, and in finding Eugene O'Neill less than completely satisfying in his. The great works of art are not to be judged like the lesser ones, and he adjusts his standards accordingly. In the land of the theater, the plains and valleys may be admired as well as the mountain peaks.

The drama is the most popular of the arts because, especially during the present age of television, it gives the greatest enjoyment to the largest number of persons. In almost every age the theater has held its own against competition; in times of war or depression attendance has fallen off scarcely at all. The Puritans closed the theaters in England during the Commonwealth, and forbade the performance of plays; but though the theaters were officially closed, the drama was kept alive by surreptitious performances that were well attended. During both world wars the theaters and motion pictures did a most thriving business. But the most remarkable phenomenon in theatrical history is television, which brings the drama to audiences of countless millions. *Antigone* in one performance on television in the United States was seen by more people than had seen it in its entire 2400-year history before that time. Eddie Cantor, commenting on the difference between slowly building up a reputation through years of patient plodding around the country before finally making it on Broadway, and the sudden bursting into fame on one nation-wide hook-up on television, tells how on one such telecast an actor may become known to more people than he, Cantor, had played to in thirty-five years of show business. The drama of every age reveals what entertained the people of that age; it also reflects what they were thinking about.

Chapter 2

WHAT IS A PLAY?

A STORY IN DRAMATIC FORM, whether it is acted in the theater or read by the individual in seclusion, is a coming to life of the characters and plot. Other writers tell their stories themselves; the playwright creates characters who live and tell their own stories. The acted play is, of course, the best example of the coming to life, but acted or not, a play has a vitality lacking in other forms of literature. The continuous use of dialogue and action, the omission of description and commentary on the part of the playwright, and the condensation and compression necessary to bring the play within the two and a half or three-hour time limit give the drama its distinctive qualities. Published versions of plays nowadays contain more and more lengthy stage directions and authors' commentaries, but these are meant for the reader; the theater audience does not need them.

With the advent of television, the drama has become more popular and widespread than ever before, and nowhere else is the coming to life better exemplified than in some of the television programs of today. Especially is this true of the so-called "documentary" play, where a newsworthy story is presented not by reporters or commentators but by actors who "dramatize" it. A family discovers strange happenings going on in its home—dishes move around, containers come open and spill, chairs slide across the floor. What is the explanation? Is it a poltergeist? Is there a natural explanation? The whole story is acted out in an hour television program. At the end of the program, the announcer introduces the real family the events happened to—in other words, first a group of actors act out the story, *dramatize* it, then we meet the real life actors, who for the sake of verisimilitude are not capable of presenting the facts convincingly! Television programs like *Divorce Court, Juvenile Court, Traffic Court,* reproduce actual cases, the judges and officers of the court are real, but the persons being tried are portrayed by actors.

Discoveries, inventions, lives of famous persons, adventures, experiences of almost every sort have been dramatized on television in ever increasing numbers. But these dramatized incidents, adventures, biographies, are not plays, although they are related to them; they are not written by expert playwrights, craftsmen of the theater, but by expert dramatizers who know how to adapt their material to the needs of television. A play is much more than a dramatic television sketch.

Most stories are based on conflict, and a play, to begin with, is the story of a conflict.* It is really written entirely in dialogue, for the stage directions are not part of the play proper. The texts of Shakespeare's plays printed in his own lifetime and for almost a century after his death contain few or no stage directions—the plays were intended for the theater, and it was up to the stage manager to arrange entrances, exits, and business; the texts look more like long narrative poems than like the printed plays familiar to us today. Most of the stage directions in Shakespeare's plays were added by the eighteenth-century editor Rowe, in an age when reading and studying of the plays was becoming increasingly popular. The story of a conflict, told entirely in dialogue, is dramatic writing as distinguished from the other chief form of storytelling, narrative.

The novelist or short story writer, although he makes frequent use of dialogue, depends for his effects on description and commentary as well as on straightforward narration. He may make his story as short or as long as he pleases. He is bound by no restriction other than his sense of proportion. The playwright, however, must tell his story within a strict time limit—the two and a half or three hours that are the ordinary length of a performance. A few playwrights have exceeded this time limit. Eugene O'Neill has written two lengthy plays, *Strange Interlude* and *Mourning Becomes Electra,* which when produced started in the late afternoon, allowed an intermission for dinner, and took up the rest of the eve-

---

* For a discussion of conflict, see Chapter 3.

ning. Shaw's *Back to Methuselah* is divided into five parts, and as first presented each part was a performance by itself; later the whole play was presented in three, instead of five, successive performances. Even longer are Hardy's *The Dynasts* and Swinburne's Mary Stuart trilogy—the latter, if the three plays are considered as one, being undoubtedly the longest play written in English. Such lengthy plays are either the result of a desire to experiment with the dramatic form, as with O'Neill and Shaw, or else they are closet drama, like *The Dynasts* and the Mary Stuart plays, and not fitted for the stage. The time limit for the playwright is a strict one, but no real reason exists for rebellion against it. If Shakespeare can tell the story of King Lear or Antony and Cleopatra within the limit, no other playwright need ever complain that he is handicapped. A very long literary work belongs to the province of the novelist, not the playwright.

No time may be wasted in a play. Not only should every speech be indispensable, but because of the condensation and compression necessary in the dramatic form, the playwright must present his material quickly, yet convincingly. The conventions of the drama are so firmly established and playwrights have perfected their technique so well that audiences usually forget how everything in a play is speeded up according to scale, as it were. A meal that in real life would last an hour or more is served, from beginning to end, in ten minutes on the stage. Conversations and discussions of some length are represented in a few lines, a battle is fought in a few minutes, a courtroom trial is presented in a few speeches. The Capulet ball at which Romeo and Juliet first meet must have lasted the better part of that exciting Sunday evening; yet the representation of it in the play lasts about five minutes. After the ball comes the famous balcony scene, which is also played in about five minutes; yet Romeo seeks Juliet immediately after the ball, they speak most of the night, and at the end of the scene Romeo goes directly to Friar Laurence's cell and finds the good father already up and about his early morning duties. In fact, the whole play is an excellent example of condensation and compression. In the narrative poem by Brooke, which was Shakespeare's source for the play, the action covers a period of five or six months; in *Romeo and Juliet* Shakespeare has cut down the time to less than four days. Coleridge's dictum about the "willing suspension of disbelief for the moment which constitutes poetic faith" applies equally well to the drama, audiences of which accept on faith many other conventions besides that of the rapid passing of time.

With the development of the picture-frame stage of modern times, as distinguished from the open-air stage of the Greek theater and the platform stage of the Elizabethan, came the convention of the fourth wall, or rather the removal of the fourth wall. No one ever saw a room with only three walls, with most of the furniture facing the open space, nor did anyone ever see a group of persons in such a room moving about and talking so as to be seen and heard to best advantage from the wall-less side of the room; yet that is exactly what one sees in almost every modern play. Some playwrights have imagined the presence of the fourth wall, but all attempts to create something to take its place have resulted only in spoiling the illusion. On the other hand, the three-walled room that the audience sees is a true to life view, as no person in a room sees the wall behind him. And the increasing use of glass in building construction today makes it quite conceivable that a person could see into a room from the outside.

The soliloquy and the aside are conventions that have come down to us from the early days of the drama, and we are still willing to accept them, within reason. Ibsen tried to banish the soliloquy from the stage as unnatural, but he did not succeed. As a matter of fact, soliloquies are fairly common in everyday life, and their use on the stage is not at all illogical. The aside is probably less common in life than the soliloquy, and is certainly more difficult to accept dramatically. The audience does not object so much to the idea that an actor is supposed to be heard throughout the auditorium, yet not to some or all the others on the stage, as to the unnaturalness of the action, which those not supposed to hear the aside would surely observe and think strange, if not downright rude. But both the aside and the soliloquy have been the stock in trade of many playwrights, and will no doubt continue to be acceptable as long as they serve their purpose.

Another difference between the playwright and the novelist or short story writer is that the playwright must take particular pains to be clear and understandable. A reader can pause to reread or ponder a passage that troubles him or over which he wishes to meditate; the amount of time devoted to reading depends entirely on himself. The audience in the theater has not that choice. A spectator of a play cannot rise in his seat to ask the actors to repeat or explain a passage that the reader, should he choose, might linger over as long as he cared to. The playwright must think, first, of his theater audiences, for his main desire is to please them; the reading public of a play is secondary. So the dialogue must be easy to follow, the situations easy to understand, and the character relationships simple to grasp.

The difference in method between the playwright and the novelist may perhaps best be illustrated by a study of the same story told in both the novel and play form. Many novels have been dramatized. The success of the dramatizations depends upon their vitality in the new medium and their satisfying of two groups in the audience—those who have read the novel and expect an adequate representation of story and characters, and those who are unfamiliar with the novel, but nevertheless have the right to expect a play complete in its own right and at the same time one that will give them a good idea of the novel. Some good examples of novels that have been made into plays are Melville's *Billy Budd,* Koestler's *Darkness at Noon,* Henry James's *Washington Square,* dramatized under the title *The Heiress,* and Thackeray's *Vanity Fair,* called *Becky Sharp* in the dramatized form. *Becky Sharp* will never supplant *Vanity Fair,* but it brought the novel to life, both for the audiences that saw the play and the actors who played the roles. Only in the drama is a story brought to life and at the same time made articulate.

The dramatic form of itself does not guarantee a good play. Closet dramatists like Browning and Shelley assumed too much understanding on the part of their audiences, with the result that their plays are good literature for the reader, but not living drama for the theater. The English closet drama of the nineteenth century was unsuccessful as drama mainly because the writers knew little about the theater and so did not write stories that could be acted well on the stage. Almost every poet of the century tried his hand at writing plays, and some are landmarks in English literature: Shelley's *The Cenci* and *Prometheus Unbound,* Byron's *Cain,* Tennyson's *Becket,* Swinburne's *Atalanta in Calydon,* Hardy's *The Dynasts;* but they are outstanding as literature, not as drama. Closet drama may be defined as literary drama that is inherently untheatrical; the closet dramatists were poets first, and playwrights only secondarily. Their laudable attempt to raise the standard of English drama, which had fallen quite low during the period, failed because they were not playwrights first and men of letters secondarily. They tried to show that drama and literature need not be separated, but oddly enough they proved just the opposite, for nowhere is the gap between the two greater than in their plays.

The playwright writes for the actor as well as for the audience. *A play is the story of a conflict, written to be enacted by performers before an audience.* Many good plays have never been acted, and the reading of plays in book form is becoming more and more popular, so that a play may be enjoyed without the benefit of a stage performance. The important thing to remember is that whether it has ever been acted or not a play is *written* so that it *could* be acted. The story told in a play may hold a reader as well as it does an audience in a theater; but it is written so that it could, at any time, under the proper conditions, come to life, "be enacted by performers before an audience."

When a play comes to life on the stage, it is a result of the collaboration of the playwright, the actor, the director, and the audience, each of whom has an important share in the making of the finished product. Once the play is written, it is the director who makes the next move in the collaboration. He must choose the actors, see that they are the right ones for the parts, train them to bring out the play's possibilities, provide the scenery and lighting effects necessary, and in general take care of the practical details of making a play come to life in the theater. The actor's share is most important, for he can make or mar the play. He must be convincing in his role, he must make the character live, he must hold the audience both by his own artistry and that of the playwright, whose interpreter he is. Last is the share of the audience, without

which no theatrical performance is complete. A dress rehearsal is
not a performance. An audience must be present, collaborating
with the actors, living the play with them, if it is to be a success.
Every actor knows the dismal feeling of playing to an audience
that is restless, inattentive, or worst of all, bored, when the play
falls flat as he tries to fight something not his own fault or that of
the playwright. Another time, with a sympathetic audience, the
same actor in the same play will give an inspired performance. A
weak link in the fourfold collaboration can spoil the best of plays;
a perfect collaboration can make even a mediocre play seem better
than it is.

The experienced reader of plays acts them out in his mind as he
reads, they come to life in his imagination, and often he may even
prefer reading to seeing them, especially if he fears that a good play
may be spoiled by a poor acting. Charles Lamb, in a well-known
essay,* went so far as to say that Shakespeare's plays were incapable of being acted on the stage, and were more satisfying when
they were read. Coming from such a lover of the theater as Lamb,
the statement seems surprising until we remember that he idealized
Shakespeare, that only a perfect performance would satisfy him,
that standards of acting had fallen low at the time, and so his own
imagination could serve him better than could the theater. Swinburne, always greatly interested in the drama and a writer of plays
throughout his long career, was so disgusted by a performance he
saw as a young man that he vowed never to visit a theater again, and
as far as we know, never did. Plays are meant for the stage, but
many true lovers of the drama prefer to keep them in the theater of
the mind.

The study of the drama necessarily deals chiefly with the printed
play. The motion pictures and television, however, are reaching
such vast audiences today that they are bound to influence the
drama of the future, perhaps to modify it considerably. A motion
picture is the collaboration of playwright, actor, and director; its
audience, far greater than that which ever saw or sees a play, does
not share in the collaboration at all. Dramatically speaking, the

* *On the Tragedies of Shakespeare.*

outstanding weakness in a picture is the absence of a bond between screen and auditorium, the inharmonious relationship between a recorded and to that extent mechanized performance and a changing, living audience. A television play, with an audience even greater than that of a picture, cuts down on the collaboration still further. Although studio audiences may be present at telecasts, the real audiences are the millions listening in at home, an entirely new kind of audience hitherto unknown. Some of the plays especially written for television have been published and make interesting reading, but on the whole the principles of drama will best be studied from the stage plays of the past and present, at first hand in the theater wherever possible, in television presentations of these plays, but largely of course from published works that have become and are becoming a permanent part of literature.

Chapter 3

CONFLICT: THE ESSENCE OF DRAMA

THE ESSENCE OF DRAMA is conflict. Every dramatic situation arises from conflict between two opposing forces. Although dramatic situations belong primarily to the theater, they are not limited to the acted or printed play but abound in literature, history, science, business, everyday life, if the observer is but keenly aware of their existence and import. To be aware of these dramatic situations is not difficult in a play, a novel, or a short story, because the writer has taken pains to make them clear. But elsewhere a situation that may seem extremely dramatic to one person will appear dull and uninteresting to another who does not know the background or realize the significance of the facts.

When the Russians sent out their first Sputnik, the whole world was interested. It was a dramatic situation as simple and obvious as any that a playwright might have arranged for the stage, for here was a dramatization of the whole struggle between a free democracy and a dictator state. When Lincoln said goodbye to the people of Springfield from the rear platform of the train that was to take him to Washington and his inaugural, most of those present must have felt the drama of the situation. But the scene assumes much greater significance as Robert Sherwood has used it to end his play *Abe Lincoln in Illinois*—as Lincoln says he does not know if he will ever return to Springfield, the train slowly pulls away, the audience hears, softly played, the strains of *His Soul Goes Marching on*, and knows that when the President does return home it will be in his coffin.

When Galileo, forced by the church to recant his statement that the earth revolved about the sun, said under his breath, "And yet it moves," there were probably few present who sensed the full

drama of the situation.* The conflict was between one man and the
world—but more than that, it was the gallant struggle of one man
who knew he was right against a world that would not listen to a
truth, a truth which we know will be accepted by succeeding ages
as obvious. It is our understanding of all the implications of the in-
cident that makes the scene so dramatic to us today.

Suppose we were guests at the home of a prominent person whom
we knew only casually, and walking through one of the rooms one
evening we saw our host kneeling as if in prayer, unaware that
standing near him, watching quietly, was a young man, his nephew.
The scene would be interesting to us, because it is somewhat unusual, but we should not find in it anything dramatic. But if we
knew the family well, and realized that the young man suspected
his uncle of having murdered his father before marrying his mother,
that this moment was the first he had had to be alone with the murderer since the murder, and that he was now wondering if he
should seize the opportunity to avenge his father's death, the scene
would be tremendously dramatic to us. What will the young man
do? We watch breathlessly for the next move. Knowing something
of the family history, we could read much more into the situation
than if we were strangers. But to understand the full significance
of the moment we have to read Shakespeare's presentation of it. The
character of Hamlet is analyzed so subtly and penetratingly as the
play progresses that we get to know him better than we know our
best friend; we watch him as he struggles against himself and
against the various forces he is obliged to fight, and when we come
to his speech

> Now might I do it pat, now he is praying;
> And now I'll do 't

we realize that he faces the most momentous decision of his life.

It is the business of the playwright to present his situation so
clearly and vividly that the conflict is immediately or almost immediately evident. The playwright must keep the idea of conflict
continually before the audience. In fact, the dramatic method of

* Historians now doubt the truth of this story, but true or not, it is an
excellent illustration of a dramatic situation. If invented, it shows the instinct
for drama characteristic of all ages.

telling a story is to set it forth in a series of dramatic situations, one following another in the order best calculated to hold the interest. Between each situation and the next is a connecting passage, a sort of pause, used for character delineation, comic interlude, or preparation for the next dramatic moment, but the main thread of the story must never be lost. Every dramatic situation represents a phase of the larger conflict that is the theme of the play.

DOMINATIVE AND DEFENSIVE FORCES IN CONFLICT

Of the two forces in dramatic conflict, one is usually stronger than the other at the beginning of the play and may be termed the dominative force. The opposing force may be termed the defensive. In order to make the struggle or conflict exciting, which is one of the synonyms of *dramatic,* the playwright must make the odds fairly even. There is not much drama in a home run for the team leading by a large score, or in a ninety-yard run by a team already winning by a large margin. The dramatic home run is hit at a crucial moment when it wins or ties the game; the dramatic touchdown comes when the score is tied or very close. When a hundred men overcome one man in a fight, the odds are too great for drama; but when one man, singlehanded, routs a hundred, *a la* Cyrano de Bergerac, drama abounds.

The two conflicting forces should, then, be so matched that the apparently weaker, the defensive, will at least theoretically have a chance to overthrow the apparently stronger, the dominative. It follows that there are two main patterns in the dramatic conflict: the dominative force remains dominative, and nothing the defensive force does affects it, although the defensive continually hopes that it will; or the dominative force is overcome by the defensive, and their positions are reversed.

Oedipus hopes to avoid the fate that has been prophesied for him. Fate is the dominative force, Oedipus the defensive. Oedipus thinks he has outwitted the gods and even thinks he can become dominative, but the dominative force never gives way. Fate is the dominative force in *Romeo and Juliet,* as we are told in the prologue. Romeo's "Oh, I am fortune's fool" at the moment he has killed Tybalt and realizes that Fate has tricked him, and his "Then I defy you, stars!" when he learns of Juliet's supposed death, shows that he knows he is the defensive force and is desperately trying to overcome the dominative. In Galsworthy's *Escape*, Matt Denant is the defensive force against the law, or society. He seems at times to be getting the better of his antagonist, but as he says at the end of the play, "It's one's decent *self* one can't escape." His training and instincts have placed him all along on the side of law and order. The dominative force has remained dominative.

In the second main pattern, the defensive force overcomes the dominative. At the beginning of *Hamlet*, Claudius is the dominative individual, Hamlet the defensive. When Hamlet learns of the murder, he immediately plans to overthrow the dominance of Claudius, who is determined to retain it. The issue is clear-cut. Hamlet eventually does overcome the dominative force and becomes finally dominant over a defensive Claudius, just before they both die. The tragedy has resulted because Hamlet has waited too long to overcome the dominance of his antagonist. The Shakesperean tragic hero overcomes his flaw, usually not in time to avert disaster, but the defensive overcomes and becomes the dominative.

In the second pattern, where the defensive overcomes the dominative force and reverses their positions, the defensive force may be a likable character striving against the dominance of a disagreeable force and eventually getting the upper hand; it may be an unjustly accused character who eventually proves his innocence; it may be the Horatio Alger type of hero, a struggling poor young man who eventually becomes a success; it may be an unpleasant person pushing his way into a society that resents him but has to accept him; it may be an evil force overcoming good.

Nora, in Ibsen's *A Doll House*, is the defensive force that finally overcomes the dominative force that has governed her life. In Howard's *The Silver Cord* the possessive mother is the dominative force, the two sons are the defensive; one son overcomes the dominance, the other does not—"engulfed forever" is the final stage direction describing the son who will all his life remain a defensive force. In Sheridan's *The School for Scandal* Joseph Surface, the hypocrite, is dominative, and his brother Charles, the spendthrift, defensive; this is only one of the conflicts in the play that the famous screen scene resolves, but after that scene Joseph, discredited, is no longer dominative, and Charles, now in favor, has changed from defensive to dominative. Lincoln, in *Abe Lincoln in Illinois*, is defensive at the beginning of the play, dominative at the end.

In addition to the two chief patterns is a combination of the two. The dominative and defensive forces reverse positions more than once. The dominative is overcome, becomes defensive for a time, then overcomes the opposition and becomes dominative again. This may go on, the fortunes of war changing from side to side, until one force definitely establishes domination over the other. The Love and Honor plays of the Restoration period provide a good illustration. Love and honor take turns being dominative; love usually takes over at the end. In Dryden's *All for Love* Cleopatra is at first defensive, then dominative; then Octavia becomes dominative, with Cleopatra defensive; then finally Cleopatra emerges the victor. Lee's *Rival Queens* follows a similar pattern. In Maugham's *The Circle*, which force will be dominative is not disclosed until the very end of the play, when Elizabeth runs off with Teddy, although an astute playgoer could probably anticipate the outcome. In Coward's *Design for Living* several shifts occur until the protagonists make up their minds. Melodrama, where the hero and the villain are alternately dominative, also illustrates the combination pattern.

The patterns are capable of numberless modifications and variations; the playwright has an almost unlimited number of situations at his disposal. A character may be dominative and defensive at the same time. Hamlet is defensive toward his chief antagonist, but he is dominative toward Ophelia, toward Polonius, toward Rosencrantz and Guildenstern; his tragedy is that dominative as he is toward most persons and situations he is defensive toward the chief dominative force opposing him. A variant pattern may have two dominative forces, like Antony and Roberts in Galsworthy's *Strife*, both defeated at the end, but not by each other. Galsworthy as usual shows his impartiality, although he represents the forces of capital and labor dominative and defensive respectively.

The defensive force may be aware of what he is fighting, or he may not—Oedipus is not aware of what he is up against, although the audience is. The defensive force that eventually overcomes the dominative may enlist our sympathies or it may not—when Lopahin buys the Cherry Orchard, are we glad of his rise, or do we feel sorry for the dominative force that has now become defensive?

Iago early becomes the dominative force over the defensive Othello. Whether we consider Othello the abused person and Iago the villain, or Othello the fool and Iago the clever one, the dominative-defensive relationship is perfectly clear in regard to the individual conflict. At the end of the play Iago has become the defensive force, but not through Othello; Othello, although overcome by Iago, at last, in a larger sense, overcomes his dominative force and regains his nobility just before he dies. In Barrie's *The Admirable Crichton* Lord Loam is in one sense dominative in the first act, Crichton is dominative in the second and third acts, and Loam in a sense resumes his dominance in the last act. Loam's dominance is artificial, however; Crichton's is real.

THE THREE TYPES OF CONFLICT

The dominative-defensive conflict may take three forms. The simplest form is that in which the two conflicting forces are centralized in two individuals. When the hero and the villain are fighting hand to hand on the edge of a cliff and the interest of the audience is concerned with the physical outcome of the battle, the playwright is presenting one of the most fundamental situations in human nature, based on the principle of self-preservation. Plays of primitive peoples, early plays of civilized nations, and the cheaper melodramas of any age make use of this first principle.

The conflict between individuals is everywhere evident in drama. Shakespeare knew the value of this elementary type of conflict and used it throughout his plays. When Hamlet fights Laertes, when Romeo fights Tybalt, when Iago is baiting Othello, when Beatrice and Benedick have their battles of wit, when Petruchio is trying to tame Katharina, the playwright is appealing to an instinct that is common to all types of audiences. This conflict of individual against individual, not restricted to the physical, of course, is as a matter of fact the basis of most dramatic situations, even though the main conflict of the play is one of the other two types.

Nora's talk with her husband in the last act of *A Doll's House;* Cyrano holding off De Guiche with the story of having just come from the moon; Dr. Faustus being pulled down to hell by Mephistophilis, in Marlowe's play; the famous "proviso" scene between Millamant and Mirabell in Congreve's *Way of the World;* Stanley brutally attacking Blanche in Williams' *A Streetcar Named Desire;* Biff Loman telling his father off and then breaking down in Miller's *Death of a Salesman,* are a few more illustrations in a list that could be extended almost indefinitely.

The second type of conflict is that between the individual and outside forces—society, the supernatural, destiny or fate. In *Oedipus the King* the conflict, as has already been said, is between Fate, which dominates men's lives, and Oedipus, who is trying to avoid what has been decided for him. Everyman is trying to ward off Death, in the medieval morality—although Death is a character in the play, and his conflict with Everyman might be considered that between individuals, the characters in the play, as in all moralities, are to be understood symbolically, so that the conflict is between individual Man and his inevitable Death, which Man tries to postpone. In Ibsen's *Enemy of the People,* the conflict is between Dr. Stockmann and the citizens of the town, or to state it in a larger way, between the reformer who is earnestly trying to better society and that society which just as obstinately refuses to be reformed. In Synge's *Riders to the Sea* the conflict is between the villagers and the sea which inexorably takes as toll the lives of those who would wrest a living from it. *The Great Galeoto,* by Echegaray, tells how public opinion, by a whispering campaign, drives a faithful wife and friend into each other's arms. They have no intentions of becoming lovers, they struggle against their fate, but in the end they succumb. *The Hairy Ape,* Eugene O'Neill's story of a man out of his natural element, Ibsen's *Peer Gynt* and *Brand* both telling of men who seemed to stand alone against the world's conventions, Marlowe's *Tamburlaine,* in which the hero contends against the world, are some of the plays based on the conflict of man against an outside force. In this conflict the individual almost invariably loses, for man as a rule does not conquer the world or overcome supernatural forces or fate.

The third type of conflict is that between the individual and himself. One of the striking examples of this type of conflict is Stevenson's *Dr. Jekyll and Mr. Hyde,* as dramatized by Thomas Henry Sullivan. Although not so effective as the original story, it is a remarkable study of the good and evil in man struggling against each other. In O'Neill's *Emperor Jones* the protagonist is, to be sure, fighting the natives he has so long mistreated, but the real conflict is between Jones and his own superstitious fears. It is not the natives who finally defeat him, but himself, and the playwright symbolizes the conflict graphically by the device of the silver bullet which ends Jones's life. In Anderson's *Elizabeth the Queen* Elizabeth must decide whether she wishes to be Queen or Woman; she has been both for a long time, then the moment comes when she must make a choice between one or the other, she tricks Essex, has him arrested; Elizabeth the Queen has triumphed, but for the rest of the play Elizabeth the Woman is a broken person—"stricken," as the playwright says in the final stage direction. The classic example of this type of conflict is, of course, Hamlet. The main conflict in the play is in Hamlet's mind.

The three types of conflict usually exist in combinations. One type will predominate, but it will rarely be the only one in a play; the subtleties of the human mind are too complex for simple treatment. Thus Hamlet's conflict is a mental one, but it is also a conflict with the king, with Rosencrantz and Guildenstern, with the queen, with Laertes, with Ophelia. The conflict of King Lear is not merely that of an aged father against two ungrateful daughters; he is also fighting for the right of old age to have some consideration at the hands of the younger generation; most important of all, the demanding, tyrannical, hot-tempered Lear is in conflict with the real Lear, who is a kind and loving father. *Everyman,* already shown to be a story of conflict between individuals or between man and an outside force (death), could also be thought of as conflict between man and himself, between man's love of life and his fear of death. The conflict between Dr. Faustus and Mephistophilis could also be interpreted as an inner conflict between the forces of good and evil in the mind of Faustus. Nora, in *A Doll's House*, is in conflict with her husband to make him understand what she has done; she is also fighting for her right to exist as an individual, not merely as a "doll" wife, and for the right of all women to lead their own lives. God, in Connelly's *Green Pastures*, is in continual conflict with the people of his earth, who persist in their wicked ways until he abandons them; then, when his people cry out to him for help, he is troubled—he says he will not listen to their pleas and yet he cannot help himself; the conflict becomes an inner conflict where God learns he also must suffer.

CONFLICT IN TERMS OF THEME AND PLOT

The statement of the conflict in any play should always be reducible to simple terms, both general and particular. *The statement of the conflict in general terms is the theme of the play; in particular terms it is the plot.* The great playwright usually thinks first of a theme, and then invents a plot to illustrate it. Some playwrights, of course, work the other way around—their first inspiration is the plot, and they write a play with no particular theme in mind. Such a play is likely to be disappointing, for we look for a theme, a main idea, in all literary compositions, though it be merely a vague expression of the author's philosophy or personality.

In *Oedipus* the general statement of the conflict is that man cannot avoid his fate. The particular statement of the conflict is that a man, hearing a prophecy that he will kill his own father and marry his mother, runs away from his home in order to avoid the fulfilment of the prophecy; but of course in trying to run away from his fate, he runs right into it. One is reminded of the Oriental tale of the Grand Vizier who asked the Sultan if he could leave town for a few days, as the Angel of Death kept looking at him in the court as if the Grand Vizier's time had come and he thought if he left the court for a few days Death would forget the matter. The Sultan gave his minister permission to leave the court, asked where he intended going, and the reply was Samarra. After the departure, the Sultan asked the Angel of Death why he was so interested in the Vizier, and Death answered that he had orders to take the gentleman the next day at Samarra, and he just wondered why the courtier was still in the court. In like manner Oedipus flees from his fate, only to meet it. Sophocles' initial idea was probably to write a play to make the point that man cannot escape his fate; the old story of the man who killed his father and married his mother then came to mind as an excellent plot to use for this theme.

The general statement of the conflict in *Hamlet* might be somewhat as follows: An introspective, meditative, studious person is suddenly faced with a situation in which his ordinary powers are of no use to him, a situation that requires a decisive action distasteful and foreign to his nature. What will happen? The statement might be even more general. A person suddenly finds that he has to do something for which he feels himself unfitted. What will happen? * The particular statement of the conflict is that a young man, inclined to think well of his fellows, devoted to his father and mother, has discovered that his uncle has seduced his mother and murdered his father. What will he do about it? The general statement of the conflict in *King Lear* is that youth and old age are ever antagonistic, especially children and aged parents. The particular statement of the conflict is that an old king, planning to divide his kingdom among his three daughters, disinherits in a fit of anger his one good daughter and gives the kingdom to his two evil daughters, with tragic results. This is the main plot. In the subplot, Shakespeare in a most daring stroke of dramatic genius gives us not a counterplot or comic relief plot but a repetition of the main plot: an old nobleman with two sons, one good and one evil, makes

* Of course the theme of *Hamlet* may be stated in more ways than one, depending on the interpretation of the play. Coleridge in one of his lectures says that "Shakespeare wished to impress upon us the truth, that action is the chief end of existence—that no faculties of intellect, however brilliant, can be considered valuable, or indeed otherwise than as misfortunes, if they withdraw us from, or render us repugnant to action, and lead us to think and think of doing, until the time has elasped when we can do anything effectually." Miss Lily B. Campbell, in her *Shakespeare's Tragic Heroes, Slaves of Passion,* calls Hamlet a study in the passion of grief. Harold Weston, in his book *Form In Literature,* says the theme is: "One defect of character may corrupt the whole man."

the same mistake as the king, disinherits the good son and favors the evil one, again with tragic results.

One of the best plays to come out of World War I was *What Price Glory?* by Maxwell Anderson and Laurence Stallings. The theme of the play, expressed in the title, is the high price war demands from both victors and losers. The conflict in general terms is that soldiers resent leaving their private lives in order to fight a war, but once in war, they are possessed with a crazy kind of fanatic zeal which overcomes their common sense. To illustrate this theme the authors show as their protagonists two men who were always fighting each other in private life, especially over women, but who were the best of friends when they were together fighting the enemy. The play leaves one with an unforgettable picture of the war. Another World War I war play, every bit as good, is R. C. Sherriff's *Journey's End,* with a somewhat similar theme. The plot is much more subdued in tone: a young officer just out of training camp joins a unit in France, and the conflict in part is between this young officer and the captain in charge of his company, who is engaged to marry the newcomer's sister. One of the best plays about World War II was *Mister Roberts,* by Thomas Heggen and Joshua Logan. The theme is that the men who perform the humdrum, unexciting, everyday tasks in the armed forces are just as necessary as those who take part in actual combat. The plot tells about Mr. Roberts, who resents being kept out of action, who finally manages to get transferred to another ship where he does see action and is killed.

In all three plays the general conflict is of course the war, a fertile field for the playwright, as it is naturally dramatic, the conflict between two fighting forces. No one play could deal with a war in its entirety (even in Hardy's *Dynasts,* perhaps the most ambitious play ever written, the conflict is centralized in the characters of Napolean, Wellington, and Nelson); therefore, the playwright presents some phase of the greater conflict in the lesser conflicts that form his plot. If we should read a number of war plays, we should find a great variety of plots, but the themes would be relatively few.

THE RELATION OF THEME AND PLOT

There is a direct relation between theme and plot. The plot must illustrate the theme, and if the play is to be convincing there must be no incongruity between the two. The theme may be dignified, even noble; but if the plot is untrue to life or exaggerated, the play will never rank among the important works, which are usually memorable for both. Hamlet's problem may be thought of in universal terms, which makes it our problem as well, but it is illustrated by a most exciting story, and we remember Hamlet, Claudius, Gertrude, Ophelia, Laertes, Polonius and the rest more vividly than we remember the general implications. *King Lear* is a treatment of one of the vital problems of human life; when we finish seeing or reading it, we are profoundly moved by the poignant situation that we realize is a common one in the world. But more than this, we also have a vivid remembrance of the old king who has been so horribly mistreated by his daughters. The theme of Galsworthy's *Strife* is the eternal conflict between capital and labor; when we look back on the play, we remember the author's conclusion—that neither capital nor labor will gain much by fighting each other. But what also stands out in our minds is the picture of the two protagonists in whom Galsworthy has centered the conflict, the capitalist and the labor leader, both of whom are broken men when the fight is over. We remember Maeterlinck's *Blue Bird* for its theme that happiness is to be found at home, but we also remember with great delight the adventures of the two children who were seeking happiness.

In *What Price Glory?* the grim background of war is never far away, but we are much more interested in the personal feud between Captain Flagg and Sergeant Quirt. Somerset Maugham's *The Circle* may be a social document with an important theme, but the clever characters who say clever things as the story unfolds are what we remember. Shaw's *Candida* may be a sermon on marriage, but the triangle story and the relationships of the three main characters are what make the play entertaining.

The plot should be a logical presentation of the theme, so that the generalization implied in the theme will hold true at the end of the play. There should not be an unfair or special case to prove a general thesis. An example of the lack of perfect fusion between theme and plot appears in Pinero's *The Second Mrs. Tanqueray.* What will happen if a man in the upper class in England marries a woman of a lower class? This theme might well be the subject of a great play; the situation is clearly one to make us think; but the plot that the playwright has invented to illustrate the theme is too special a case to convince us. We do not feel that the play is the final word on the subject. The plot may be stated briefly as follows: What will happen if a man in the upper classes of society marries a woman of the lower classes, *if* the woman has had a "past," and *if* the man has a daughter (by previous marriage) who suddenly announces her engagement to a man who is revealed as a former lover of the woman? The plot of the play immediately becomes a very special case, and does not give us the feeling of universality that we expected from the theme. Many plays are thus weakened because their authors have not invented a fitting plot for their theme.

If we compare the theme with the plot of Anne Nichols's *Abie's Irish Rose,* one of the most commercially successful plays ever produced, we may perhaps see why the play was so popular with a certain public and at the same time incurred the scorn of virtually all the critics. The theme of the play is a good one: What will happen when an Irish girl marries a Jewish boy? This theme would obviously have a wide popular appeal, because the problems it suggests are continually met in life. But the plot is so utterly commonplace, the characters are so clearly types, and the comedy is of such a cheap order that the result naturally disgusted the critics, although the appeal of the play, and especially its true-to-type humor, as naturally caught the fancy of the public.

More numerous than plays with good themes and trivial or ill-fitting plots are plays with good plots and trivial themes. Perhaps the most generally heard criticism of modern drama is that the playwright does not deal with dignified and elevated themes, that there are exceptions, of course, but that on the whole modern drama does not take itself seriously enough. The answer to such criticism, which has probably been made in every age of dramatic history, is that great plays do not appear in large numbers, and that the proportion of serious plays in our own time is probably as large as that in any other period.

Certainly many playwrights of today are to be taken seriously. Sartre's existentialism shows through all his plays; Shaw is a reformer whose prefaces to the plays must be read carefully; Ionesco sees life symbolically and forces us to see through the symbols; Pirandello shows us reality and illusion side by side and challenges us to tell them apart. Among United States' playwrights O'Neill never lost sight of his two main contentions, that life is full of frustrations, that illusions of happiness are the nearest we can get to happiness, and that if we haven't learned in two thousand years that spiritual matters are more important than material ones, we had better give the world back to the ants. Maxwell Anderson put it that good men go down and the rats inherit the earth. And Tennessee Williams replied to a question about *A Streetcar Named Desire* regarding Blanche's breakdown at the end of the play that Blanche represented refinement and culture and that if we were not careful the Stanleys of the world would take over.

At the same time it is true that there are many playwrights today with a technique superior to that of their predecessors (that is, according to our present conception of technique) who do not deal with really important and universal themes. Noel Coward will serve as representative of the group. He is extremely clever, his dialogue is amazingly dexterous, his plots are interesting and hold the attention, but when we finish seeing or reading a play of his, we are likely to ask ourselves, "What of it?" Has the playwright treated of any deep emotional experience? Has he considered any of the important problems that confront human beings? Are we to take the philosophy of life suggested in *Design for Living* or *Private Lives* seriously? The answer is obvious—and Mr. Coward himself, perhaps, would be the last person in the world to claim greatness for his plays. That they are good entertainment is beyond question; but the important plays of the world do more than entertain.

The playwright, then, must co-ordinate his theme and plot. If he stresses the theme too much and neglects the plot, we have the thesis or propaganda play in its worst form. *Damaged Goods,* by

Eugene Brieux, is a good example of the thesis stressed out of all proportion to the plot, which becomes little more than a preachment against the evils of venereal disease. Ibsen's *Ghosts,* which has as a secondary theme the same idea, so skillfully blends it into the plot that the play is a recognized masterpiece. The two plays afford an excellent study in the relationship of theme and plot: one is almost forgotten today except by students of social science; the other has become an important dramatic work of art and is still being acted. Another good example of a play in which theme is everything is that old favorite by T. S. Arthur, *Ten Nights in a Barroom;* we remember it today not for its plot but for its sermonizing, amusing to many of us now, on the evils of drinking. Bertolt Brecht's *The Private Life of the Master Race,* and Clifford Odets' *Waiting for Lefty* are two good propaganda plays in that the themes and plots fit well together, but both plays have too much preaching to please the discriminating.

At the other extreme is the play that is all plot and has no theme. There are two types, one built around situation, the other around character. Melodrama is perhaps the best example of the first type. The author has some general notion of morality to give his audience, such as the triumph of virtue and the inevitable punishment of vice, but the emphasis in the play is on the type-characters and the situations in which they find themselves, and at the end of such a play the audience is left with a feeling that it has witnessed not life but merely some exciting moments in the lives of characters that are forgotten as soon as the curtain has come down on the last act. The conflict is of the most primitive sort, with few subtle implications.* The other type is the play loosely built around one character, usually likable, who figures in a series of adventures. Examples are *Life with Father,* by Lindsay and Crouse, which holds the record for having the longest run in the history of the American theater, and *The Man Who Came to Dinner,* by Kaufman and Hart. The chief attraction in these plays was in the acting of the stars for whom the plays were intended. Incidentally, both plays were based on real life characters. The success and popularity of

* For a further discussion of melodrama see p. 126.

the plays were deserved and understandable, but they must not mislead us.

Conflict is the essence of drama, and if a play is to rank among the important plays it must have conflict worthy of consideration in both theme and plot.

Chapter 4

THE STRUCTURE OF A PLAY

LIKE ALL ARTISTS, the playwright is as much interested in the form and structure of his composition as he is in the matter with which it deals. The longer we study, the more familiar we become with any art, the more we are struck with the importance the artist gives to form. When a musician criticizes a musical work, he is likely to talk not so much about what the composer was trying to say as about how he was trying to say it; he is less concerned with theme and melody than with their development and variations, with counterpoint and harmony, with the fitness of the material for the instrument that is to play it. When a painter criticizes a painting, he is usually less interested in the subject than in the composition and balance of the work; he will cover up the right half of the picture to see if the left half has balance by itself, he will reverse the procedure, he will do the same with the upper and lower halves, he will turn the picture upside down; he will speak of color harmony, design, pattern, the method of achieving the result rather than of the result itself. Enjoyment of any work of art increases with one's understanding and appreciation of the technique that shapes it into being.

The keenest and most satisfying enjoyment of the drama is experienced by those who know enough about dramatic technique to appreciate the art with which a play is put together. Such playgoers or readers enjoy more than the story the playwright has to tell, or the theme behind the story. They find pleasure in the characterization, in the efficient use of dialogue both to entertain and to move the story along, in the building up of a dramatic situation, in the preparation for the big dramatic moments in the play, in the skill with which the complications are made to pile up and are then smoothed out, in the manner in which the forces and characters are shown to be dominative or defensive, in the fresh and original treatment of ideas and situations that have been used a thousand times before. An analysis of a work of art is not a tearing down, as some consider it, but a careful examination of the parts, for a fuller and better understanding of the whole.

ACTS AND SCENES

A play is divided into acts, which may or may not be subdivided into scenes. In French and German drama any entrance or exit of any character marks the end of a scene, and in English and American drama we retain that meaning of the word when we speak for example of Hamlet's scene with Ophelia, of the scene between Lear and Cordelia when she refuses to flatter him, or of Othello's death scene. The more general meaning in England and America is that of a subdivision of an act, when the curtain falls to indicate either a change of setting or a lapse of time or both.

The tradition that a play must have five acts, current in French classical drama and in English drama until well into the nineteenth century, was derived from the Greeks, whose tragedies consisted of five episodes, separated by odes.* An episode in a Greek play, however, is really like a modern scene rather than like an act, so that the traditional five-act structure, which influenced most of our best drama of the past, is based on a misconception. Greek tragedies were always presented on the Greek stage in threes, the trilogy telling one complete story; the production was therefore a sort of three-act play, each act having five (sometimes six) * scenes. The trilogy was always followed by a satyr play, or afterpiece. What the Greek audiences saw when they went to the theater were not five-act plays at all.

A natural number of acts for a play is three or four, and most modern plays have that number. In a three-act play the first act contains the introduction, exposition, beginning of the rising action, and the complications; the second act continues the rising action and develops the plot by furthering the complications or

* For a discussion of Greek tragedy, see p. 60.

adding new ones; the third act contains the turning point, the climax, the clearing up of the complications, and the ending. In a four-act play the third act usually contains the turning point; the climax and clearing up are reserved for the last act. The five-act play, with the turning point in the third act (the Shakespearean formula calls for the turning point in the middle of the play), has an obvious weak spot—the fourth act. That Shakespeare was aware of the weak link in the chain, with the danger of a lapse of interest on the part of the audience, is apparent in the special care he took to bolster up the fourth act with something striking or effective. In *Hamlet* it is the madness of Ophelia and the return of Laertes; in *Julius Caesar* it is the quarrel between Brutus and Cassius and the appearance of Caesar's ghost to Brutus; in *Romeo and Juliet* it is Juliet's scene before she takes the sleeping potion. Shakespeare is most skillful in giving us effective scenes called into being as a result of a technical exigency. In a three- or four-act play such scenes would either be unnecessary or else would be incorporated with others.

Whether an act has one scene or many, it is usually a unity in itself, and not an arbitrary break in the telling of the story to give the audience a breathing spell. George Bernard Shaw's *Getting Married* is a full-length comedy written as one act, but when it was presented on the stage one long sitting was considered too much for the average audience, and so for the sake of convenience two acts were made out of one. But neither act was a unity; the break was purely artificial. Ordinarily when a playwright begins to shape his ideas into play form, he finds his material quite naturally resolving itself into the various acts. Certain situations obviously belong in the first act, others in the second, and so on; the pattern of the play is clear before the actual writing starts.

Some plays seem broken up into divisions larger than acts. In Shakespeare's *Winter's Tale* the fourth act takes place sixteen years after the third, so that the play has two parts, the first three acts forming part one, the last two acts part two. In Augustus Thomas's *The Copperhead* the play is divided into two epochs, each having two acts; the second epoch takes place forty years after the first. In Rostand's *Cyrano* the last act takes place fifteen years after the preceding. In such plays we should be aware of the larger unit intended by the playwright, for obviously the careful playwright plans these breaks just as naturally as he plans his acts.

The number of scenes in a play may vary greatly. The Elizabethan or "panorama" type of play had a succession of many, in keeping with the platform stage, which made a change of scene simple, and the wide sweep of the story, which made a procession of them necessary. Shakespeare's *Antony and Cleopatra* has forty-two scenes, a large number for a five-act play; Dryden's *All for Love*, telling the same story, is at the opposite extreme, with the same setting for all five acts and no division into scenes. Modern playwrights, for practical reasons, write plays that require few changes of setting, and the general practice today is to have only one or two scenes to an act.

THE FIRST ACT

The beginning of any literary work is most important, and the playwright especially must take pains to begin well. "Make your first act clear," was the advice of the elder Dumas to his son, "your last act short, and the whole interesting." To make his first act clear the playwright must do two things: he must establish the atmosphere of the play and introduce the characters. To make the act interesting he must start the plot.

The atmosphere should be established early in the first act. The audience should know almost at the outset what kind of play it is going to witness—romance, comedy of manners, fantasy, period play, problem play, history; before the end of the act the playwright should have indicated whether the play is to be lighthearted or serious, gay or somber, flippant or sincere. The first act should indicate quite clearly whether the play will be comedy or tragedy, for in any literary composition worthy of the name of art the end is implicit in the beginning.

The openings of Shakespeare's plays are well worth study for their creation of atmosphere. The witches' scene in *Macbeth* stresses at once the supernatural element of the play. The opening scene in *Hamlet*, midnight on a platform before the castle, shows the guard not only chill with bitter cold, but also "sick at heart"; the appearance of the ghost hints that there is something seriously wrong at the court. *Romeo and Juliet* opens with a street fight between the Capulet and the Montague factions that reveals immediately and vividly the bitter enmity between the two families. The first speech in *Antony and Cleopatra* mentions "this dotage of our general's" and "the triple pillar of the world transform'd into a strumpet's fool." The historical plays usually begin with references to weighty matters of state. *Much Ado* opens on a gay note, *The Merchant of Venice* on a serious one.

The first act as a rule introduces most of the characters of the play, making clear which are the principal and which the minor ones. A character may be introduced in one of two ways: other characters may talk about him, preparing the audience for his entrance, or the character may enter without any previous mention. Usually the dominant note in the character's personality is sounded early in the act. It is instructive to note how Shakespeare makes the first utterances of his main characters significant. Hamlet's first words are an aside (also significant):

A little more than kin, and less than kind.

When Romeo enters and Benvolio says, "Good morrow, cousin," Romeo heaves a deep sigh, and then says, "Is the day so young?" His whole attitude shows his lovesick feeling for Rosaline. Lear's first speech is a command barked at Gloucester; his second shows his imperious nature, his love for Cordelia, his desire for flattery and praise. Falstaff's first words are:

Now, Hal, what time of day is it, lad?

and his intimacy with the prince is immediately evident. Beatrice's first words, "I pray you, is Signior Mountanto returned from the wars or no?" show that she thinks of Benedick more than she cares to confess. *Richard III* opens with Gloucester in a long speech that perfectly reveals his character:

Now is the winter of our discontent
Made glorious summer by this sun of York.

In *Cyrano,* Christian's fourth speech is,

You who turn into ditties Town and Court, stay by me; you will be able to tell me for whom it is I am dying of love!

His next speech:

I fear . . . ah, I fear to find she is fanciful and intricate! I dare not speak to her, for I am of a simple wit. The language written and spoken in these days bewilders and baffles me. I am a plain soldier . . . shy, to boot.

not only reveals his character but foreshadows the story in which he is to play a part. Later in the act Cyrano is introduced, in the most exciting entrance for a hero in modern drama. He has been mentioned or referred to about a dozen times; a wager is laid on his appearance; will he make good his boast to prevent the actor Montfleury from speaking on the stage? Soon Montfleury enters and begins to recite—and still no Cyrano. Suddenly a voice booms forth:

Rogue! Did I not forbid you for one month?

The playwright has not only surprised the audience, but has combined the introduction of his leading character with a dramatic situation, thus showing himself a master of technique. It will be noticed that the introduction of Cyrano is held back until almost the middle of the act—such an entrance would be spoiled by having it too near the beginning.

A good first act will contain the beginning of the plot and some of the plot movement. But as the beginning of the play is rarely the beginning of the story, the playwright must in some way tell us all that we need to know of what happened before the play opens. The manner in which he gives the necessary facts reveals whether or not he is a skillful artist, for if the spectator or reader realizes that he is merely being fed information, he is likely to become restless or bored. The playwright must devise various ways of revealing the retrospect so that it will not be too perceptible as a device but will seem a natural part of the dialogue.

When the butler, polishing the silver, and the maid, dusting the furniture, tell each other that the master, who has been away on his honeymoon, is returning that very day with his bride, they are obviously speaking to the audience. If the maid asks such questions as, "How long is it since Mr. Jones left?" and the butler answers her with the necessary retrospect, the technique is poor. We know that two servants, in possession of the facts, would not talk in this summarizing way at any time. If the maid is new in the household (an old device), and the butler is explaining matters, the technique is still obvious. A more natural way of revealing retrospect is to combine it with action. For example, as the servants are working, they wonder if everything is in proper order; will the master be satisfied? has he changed much since his marriage? will the bride like them or not?

None of these beginnings is very good. Ibsen's *Hedda Gabler* begins with Tesman and his bride just come home from their honeymoon. The opening scene is the morning after their arrival. The speakers are Tesman's aunt and the servant:

MISS TESMAN (*Stops close to the door, listens, and says softly*): Upon my word, I don't believe they are stirring yet!
BERTA (*Also softly*): I told you so, Miss. Remember how late the steamboat got in last night. And then, when they got home!—good Lord, what a lot the young mistress had to unpack before she got to bed.
MISS TESMAN: Well, well—let them have their sleep out. But let us see that they get a good breath of the fresh morning air when they do appear. (*She goes to the glass door and throws it open.*)

Notice how quickly and economically the story gets under way. Ibsen is especially noteworthy for the naturalness with which he brings in the retrospect.

Action is an essential element in a good first act. Sometimes the movement of a play is scarcely noticeable, as in Chekhov; sometimes it is boisterous and rowdy, as in a rough-and-tumble farce; but it is almost inconceivable to think of a dramatic situation without action to precede or follow it. The first act of *Romeo and Juliet* is full of action. The fight in the street is a vivid presentation of atmosphere; but more than that, it is a dramatizing of the feud.

Where a lesser playwright might have talked about the feud through the characters, Shakespeare shows it to us objectively, so that we see for ourselves. In this way the playwright catches the attention of the audience at the very beginning of the play, and at the same time makes the feud realistic and convincing. When Romeo decides to attend the Capulet ball, the plot movement definitely starts. Next we see Romeo and his friends on their way to the ball. The ball itself is a scene of action. Romeo sees Juliet, Tybalt is furious at Romeo's presence and swears revenge, Romeo and Juliet speak to and fall in love with each other. The act ends, and we wonder what will happen next.

The audience, at the end of the first act, should be eagerly looking forward to the continuation of the play. The playwright must do more than create atmosphere, introduce characters, and start the story. He must create suspense. In other words, the first act should indicate the conflicts in the play, so that the audience, waiting for the second act, should be saying to itself, "The hero is faced with such and such a problem. What will he do about it?" Just as the retrospect is that part of the story which has occurred before the start of the play, so the *prospect*, as we may call it for want of a better term, is that part occurring after but hinted at in the first act. The mention or hint, either direct or indirect, of future action is perhaps the most important element of all in the building up of a good first act.

When Hamlet tells the ghost that he will sweep to his revenge, and yet at the end of the act says,

> The time is out of joint: O cursed spite,
> That ever *I* was born to set it right!

we appreciate his difficulty, and we look forward expectantly to the mental struggle that we know will end disastrously. In *She Stoops to Conquer,* the direct prospect is that young Marlow is coming to the Hardcastle home as a suitor to Kate, and that Tony is sending him and his friend Hastings to the house as an inn. There is some indirect prospect, too—Marlow's shyness with women except those of a lower social station than his own, coupled with Kate's habit of dressing simply in the evenings, Constance Neville's pretending to be in love with Tony when she is really in love with

Hastings (this is sub-plot)—which gives a further indication of what is to come.

A good illustration of prospect is in the first act of Wilde's *Lady Windermere's Fan*. It is Lady Windermere's birthday, and she is to hold a reception. Lord Windermere asks her to invite a certain Mrs. Erlynne, a lady who has not moved in the best circles and has not been received in the best society because of her past. There is some retrospect, hinted at, which connects Mrs. Erlynne and Lord Windermere. Lady Windermere refuses to send the invitation, whereupon he sends it himself. She then threatens to insult Mrs. Erlynne if she appears at the reception. Picking up her fan, she says,

You gave me this fan today; it was your birthday present. If that woman crosses my threshold, I shall strike her across the face with it.

But this is not all the prospect. A few moments later, when Lord Windermere is on the stage alone, he says,

My God! What shall I do? I dare not tell her who this woman really is. The shame would kill her.

And the curtain falls. William Archer says that at this point a five-pound note would not have bribed him to leave the theater without seeing the second act.*

In *The Second Mrs. Tanqueray*, Aubrey Tanqueray is going to marry again because he is lonely; his first marriage had been an unhappy one, his daughter had always been cold and distant toward him and had lately announced her intention of becoming a nun, and he thinks that Paula, even though she comes from a lower social station and has had a past, will be a pleasant companion and make his life happy. The prospect is general, and provocative enough to provide a thoughtful play in the succeeding acts. But Pinero injects some direct prospect near the end of the act— Aubrey has announced his forthcoming marriage and is prepared to lose his friends for Paula's sake, Paula herself has been introduced to us, and then Aubrey finds a letter that he has not noticed before:

"My dear father,—A great change has come over me. I believe my mother in Heaven has spoken to me, and counseled me to turn to you in

* William Archer, *Play-Making* (Boston, Small, Maynard, 1912), p. 179.

your loneliness. At any rate, your words have reached my heart, and I no longer feel fitted for this solemn life. I am ready to take my place by you. Dear father, will you receive me?—Ellean."

When Paula re-enters, he "stares at her as if he hardly realized her presence." Then he recovers himself, escorts her out of the room, and the act ends. The final touch has added an entirely new complication to the problem, and we look forward with keen interest to what will happen next.

THE RISING ACTION

Having laid the groundwork in the first act, the playwright is now ready to proceed with the development of his story. The rising action starts in the first act, as a rule; it is usually the main concern of the second act. Action arising from the situation at the opening of the play, complications caused by the conflicting forces, heightening of the struggle between the forces, preparation for and leading up to the decisive clash between the two forces constitute rising action.

In *Hamlet* the action starts when Hamlet learns from the Ghost that the late king had been murdered by Claudius. This is in Act I, scene v. The first four scenes established the atmosphere, introduced the characters, and give the necessary information about the past and the situation at present; the introduction being over, we are ready for the story to begin. When Hamlet first hears the news of his father's murder he says he will take action immediately against the murderer, but a little later, at the end of the act, he is already wondering about his fitness for the task he has set himself. When the second act opens, two months have passed, and he has done nothing. The rising action in this act shows his impatience with himself for his delay, his inability to explain to himself why he cannot do the thing he knows he must do; it also shows the king becoming more and more suspicious, as he tries to discover how much Hamlet knows. At the end of the act Hamlet decides to have the players give a play that he hopes will trap the king. The rising action continues in the third act, up to the moment when Claudius betrays himself at the play.

In *Romeo and Juliet* the rising action, which begins when Romeo decides to go to the Capulet ball, continues through the ball scene, the balcony scene, the arrangements for the marriage, the marriage itself, and Tybalt's search for Romeo, ending with the duel between Tybalt and Romeo. In *She Stoops to Conquer* the rising action shows Marlow and Hastings coming to the Hardcastle home and mistaking it for an inn. The second act of *Lady Windermere's Fan* shows the reception and the arrival of Mrs. Erlynne. In the second act of *The Second Mrs. Tanqueray*, Aubrey and Paula are shown, married and settled down, in their country home. In all these examples it will be seen that the prospect of the first act is the basis, in part or entirely, of the rising action, which, if the play is to have unity, must follow logically from what has gone before.

THE TURNING POINT

The rising action ends with the turning point. In fact, the main purpose of rising action is to lead up to the turning point, or crisis, the most significant dramatic situation in the play. The playwright, as has already been said, tells his story in a series of dramatic situations, each of which is a clash between the dominative and defensive forces. The turning point is the most decisive clash between the forces, the moment at which the dominative force decisively establishes its superiority, or decisively loses it to the defensive force, which then becomes dominative. Further clashes may occur but the action has taken a definite direction toward the ending. The question in the mind of the audience at the end of the first act, "The hero is faced with such and such a problem. What will he do about it?" is beginning to be answered. The final answer, of course, is at the climax, which begins to come into direct view for the first time at the turning point.

The turning point of *Romeo and Juliet* is the killing of Tybalt. Up to this time fate has been kind to the lovers; the difficulties in their way have been smoothed out, and when they are married at the end of Act II we are almost persuaded that everything will turn out well after all. Love has been the dominative force. But the death of Tybalt changes matters, and from now on everything goes wrong. The forces against the lovers become dominant; Romeo senses this the moment he has killed Tybalt, when he says, "O, I am fortune's fool!" The fight between Romeo and Tybalt is the most decisive clash between the Capulets and Montagues; up to this point the action of the play has run in one direction; now it takes a turn and goes in another direction, toward the tragic ending.

The turning point of *Hamlet* has been variously placed, by competent critics, in the play scene, where Hamlet is fully convinced that the King is guilty of murder; in the scene where Hamlet fails to kill the King, who is kneeling in prayer; and in the scene in the Queen's closet, when the Ghost appears the second time to Hamlet. The difference of opinion is evidence of the complexity of structure of the play, which is based on several conflicts, carefully interwoven, each of which has clashes between two opposing forces. If the main conflict is considered that of the opposing wills of Hamlet and the King, the most decisive clash is in the play scene, at which the King gives himself away. Up to this point the King has been the dominative force; from now on he is on the defensive, and Hamlet becomes stronger and stronger. If the main conflict is considered to be within Hamlet himself, centering on his inability to perform an action that is extremely foreign to his nature, the turning point is his failure to kill the King when he has the opportunity. One part of Hamlet's mind is desperately anxious to kill the king, another part hesitates, holds the other part back. This second force dominates, and at the decisive moment, Hamlet does not strike; his inability to kill the king remains dominative, and the delay is fatal. Finally, if Hamlet is considered to be the victim of melancholia, the main conflict is his fight against the disease, the crisis of which is at the second appearance of the Ghost, when the melancholia, which has been dominative, suddenly leaves and Hamlet is now dominative over it. There is only one, not three turning points in *Hamlet*, but the placing of the most decisive clash between the opposing forces depends on our interpretation of the chief conflict.

The turning point in *Julius Caesar* is Brutus's good-natured but ill-advised permission to Antony to address the populace over the dead body of Caesar. The innate nobility and generosity of Brutus gives Antony his chance to sway the people against the conspirators, whose cause, which had up to now been dominative, steadily declines as the Antony force takes over the dominance. In *Othello* the turning point is in Act III, scene iii, when Iago, still pretending to be Othello's friend, finally persuades him that Desdemona is faithless, and Othello's raging jealousy becomes dominative. In *Macbeth* it is the escape of Fleance, whom Macbeth had planned to murder—"But now I am cabin'd, cribb'd, confin'd, bound in to saucy doubts and fears." The witches' prophecy that Banquo's children would be kings now haunts him more and more, the tide turns from this point, and Macbeth's fortunes, which had been dominative, begin to decline.

In *The Second Mrs. Tanqueray*, the turning point is Paula's meeting with Captain Ardale, who has become engaged to Ellean. At this moment Paula's past catches up with her, and she realizes that she is doomed; her past and all it meant, that she had thought she had dominated, will now dominate her, and eventually lead to her suicide. In *A Doll's House* it is the sudden realization on Nora's part of her husband's real character; from this point on she is no longer the doll wife but the awakened woman, and she becomes the dominative force for the rest of the play. In Anderson's *Elizabeth the Queen* the turning point is Elizabeth's crucial decision to remain a queen instead of a woman; when the test comes, her queenship is dominant, and she orders the arrest of Essex. Her womanly instincts have become definitely secondary. In Chekhov's *The Cherry Orchard* the turning point is Lopahin's announcement that *he* has bought the cherry orchard; the Ranevsky family which had been dominant for so long has lost out, and the former slave is the new owner, or in other words, the old order in Russia has lost out to the new, which will now take over. In O'Casey's *The Plough and the Stars* Jack Clitheroe must either heed his wife and remain with her, or go fight for the Nationalist cause; as Nora puts it, which is stronger, your love for me or your vanity as a military officer? When he chooses to join the fighters, O'Casey shows us that nationalism has become dominant over humanitarianism. In Shaw's *Saint Joan* the turning point is Joan's recantation of her recantation—she has signed the statement that her voices were false, that the Church was right and she was wrong, but when she is then told that she must be imprisoned for the rest of her life, that she must lose her freedom, she tears up the paper, saying she knows her voices were right, that those who are torturing her are wrong. Her natural instincts, not always dominative, now assert their final dominance.

To understand the turning point of a play is to understand the play. It is the crucial moment. It has been in the playwright's mind from the beginning (some writers conceive the "big scene" before anything else, and build the play around it), and he carefully leads up to it and away from it. The turning point must concern the main character, it must follow logically from the rising action and lead directly to the climax, it must be the decisive clash in the plot, and it must also represent the crisis in the general conflict that expresses the theme.

THE FALLING ACTION

That part of the play between the turning point and the climax is called, somewhat inappropriately, the falling action. The term is inappropriate because it implies a falling off in interest, which of course is far from the mind of any playwright. The German critic Freytag first used the phrase as a balance to rising action in his diagram of the action of a play

still accepted as standard today. The diagram has its uses, if rightly understood, and will serve until a better is found. But the only type of play it really represents is the Shakespearean, with the turning point in the middle and the rising and falling action of about equal length. A somewhat modified diagram will give a better idea of Shakespeare's usual form of play:

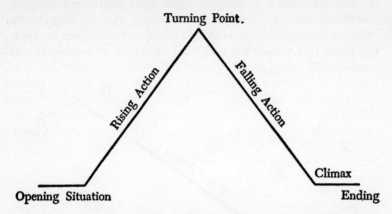

The Elizabethan "panorama" formula allowed for a fuller treatment of the story than was possible on the Greek stage or has been thought necessary on the modern stage.

The Greek dramatic formula confined the action of the play to one day, so that the rising action of the story was not told directly by the playwright but indirectly through characters or by the chorus. The Greek playwright, therefore, stressed the falling action, so that the diagram of the entire story of a Greek play would be presented thus:

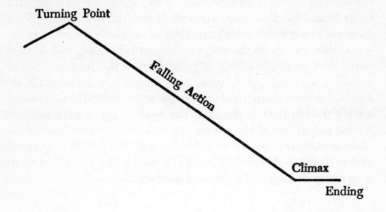

Structurally, however, a Greek play is like most plays, with the turning point either near the middle or after. In the *Agamemnon* the turning point is in the third episode, in *Oedipus* it is in the fourth. Modern plays deal mostly with rising action, ending shortly after the turning point, placing the climax, therefore, near the turning point (sometimes the two coincide), and dispensing almost entirely with falling action:

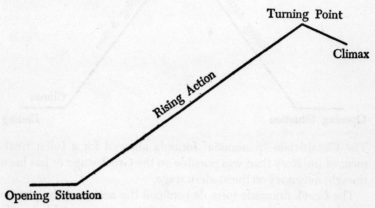

The broad scope of the Elizabethan play, the emphasis on falling action of the Greeks, with the consequent careful consideration of the results following the turning point, and the modern method of building up to the climax and stopping with much of the story left untold, are characteristic of the ages in which the plays were produced. The drama is an expression of the age in which it appears, in its form as well as in its content. It was natural for the Elizabethans, living in a free and easy time of national expansion, to demand that a story on the stage be told in full detail, and so their plays give as much action as possible directly, in a number of scenes. The Greeks, philosophic and reflective, were naturally restrained in their drama, and were more interested in the outcome of a story than in the introduction. The modern age is a restless one, we are not so sure of our values as previous ages were, and so our plays usually end not with finality but with the action suspended, and with the audience left to supply the ending according to its own interpretation of the problem involved.

THE CLIMAX

Although the action takes a turn at the turning point, the interest of the reader or spectator steadily mounts until the moment of climax, somewhere near the end of the play. Structurally the action may be represented by a broken line, as we have just seen. Emotionally the interest may be represented thus:

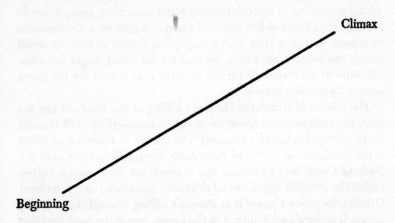

The climax is the moment of highest interest in the play. It is placed at or near the end, because anything after it is a letdown. It may be an expected action or it may be a complete surprise, but emotionally it is the end of the story, the answer to the questions raised in the first act. After the climax the playwright simply gathers up the loose ends, disposes of his characters as quickly as possible, and brings the play to a close.

A confusion of terms has existed, in the minds of some critics, between turning point and climax. The crucial moment, the point at which the rising action turns to become falling action, has often been called the climax, as a result of the diagram that shows the turning point as the apex. But the turning point is not the highest point of interest in a play, else in a Shakespearean play, for instance, interest would decline from the middle onward, an effect which does not occur. An analogy may help to make the distinction clear.

The turning point in a man's career would be that action or event that ultimately leads to failure or success—winning the first big law case or successfully performing the first big surgical operation, deciding to become a criminal by an embezzlement or a forgery, choosing between retaining a throne or marrying for love. The climax to the lawyer's career might be his appointment to the bench of the Supreme Court; that of the doctor's the saving of the life of some personage after everyone else had failed, or perhaps nation-wide recognition at the celebration commemorating many years of service; the climax of the criminal's career might be a life sentence to prison; that of a king who gave up his throne so that he could marry the woman on whom he had set his heart might be some subsequent achievement for his country that would list his name among its greatest heroes.

The climax of *Hamlet* is Hamlet's killing of the King. At last we have the answer to the question of the first act—What will Hamlet do to avenge his father's murder? The climax of *Romeo and Juliet* is the death of the lovers; of *King Lear*, the death of Lear over the body of Cordelia; of *Othello,* the magnificent final speech (often called the greatest speech in all dramatic literature) and suicide of Othello; in *Julius Caesar* it is Brutus's killing himself. In *A Doll's House* it is Nora's walking out of the house, one of the most thrilling climaxes in drama. In *Escape* it is Matt's giving himself up to the police. In *Death of a Salesman* it is Willy's suicide. The climax, being the moment of highest interest, must be worthy of its important position in the play. If it is second in significance as a dramatic situation to the turning point, it is often more thrilling or exciting. Whether a surprise or not, it must be logical and convincing, and must justify the audience's expectancy.

THE ENDING

The ending is bound up with the climax, which of course affects it directly. Technically the ending is that part of the play following the climax. It is usually short, and its purpose is mainly to bring the audience back to earth from an emotional height. Some modern playwrights stop the play at the climax, but the abrupt ending is always a shock to the audience, and it is better to have a moment or two of relaxation before the curtain falls.

After Hamlet kills the king he ascends the throne and utters his farewell; then he dies, Fortinbras enters, and the play ends with a death march. After the death of Romeo and Juliet there is a long recapitulation of the story by Friar Laurence, and the two enemy houses are finally reconciled. It has been the custom, in modern productions of these plays, to end with the death of Hamlet and of Romeo and Juliet, but lately the fashion seems to be changing to the ending as originally written. The death march adds an impressive touch to *Hamlet;* the reconciliation of the Capulets and Montagues is a necessary part of the story, else Shakespeare would not have added it. At the end of *King Lear* the government of the kingdom is given to Albany and Edgar, and England is assured of a peaceful and just reign. In *A Doll's House*, after Nora has gone, her husband is left wondering what the future will bring. In *Escape,* Matt tells the parson that it is not only the law, but one's decent *self* one cannot escape. In *Death of a Salesman,* Willy's funeral is a very inauspicious occasion; like everything else in Willy's life, even his funeral was a failure.

More generally the ending is thought of as the last part of the play, including the climax and perhaps even earlier passages. It is in this sense that we use the word when we speak of a happy or a sad ending. Whether the ending be happy or tragic is not nearly so important as that it be logical. If the direction of the falling action is toward tragedy, a sudden change in the last few moments in order to make a happy ending where it is really out of place is not only illogical and inartistic, but is untrue to life and therefore difficult for a critical audience to accept. A good example of a logical ending occurs in *The Cassilis Engagement*, by St. John Hankin. A young man, of good social standing, has fallen in love with and become engaged to a girl of the lower classes. The mother of the young man, knowing that trying to talk her son out of a marriage that she feels can bring happiness to neither will make him only the more determined to go ahead, invites the girl to visit them at their country home, that he may observe her in the company of his own family and friends. The experiment is a success as far as the mother is concerned, the girl proving to herself and to the young man that she does not belong in his set. Many writers might have been tempted to provide the usual "happy ending" to such a story—the young couple marry in spite of everything, love is superior to social station, and all turns out well. Hankin carries the story through to its logical and common-sense ending—facing the facts of the difference in their training and environment, the two separate, as they probably would in real life. Severely criticized for his unhappy ending, the playwright ably defended himself, pointing out that marriage would have brought unhappiness, and that the breaking of the engagement was the true happy ending.* Whether or not the ending was a happy one, it followed logically from the premises laid down in the play.

Too many playwrights begin a play well and end it badly. They often create a situation and then are afraid to face, or let their characters face, the consequences. If, instead of dodging the issue, they meet it squarely and courageously, the ending will come naturally. Only the most thoughtless and unsophisticated of audiences or readers, for instance, would wish a happy ending for *Romeo and Juliet*. The tragic story of a love thwarted by fate would lose all its beauty and meaning if the lovers were to live. If Hamlet were left alive at the end of the play the whole significance would be lost. On the other hand, there are some illogical endings even in Shakespeare. Why Helena, in *All's Well that Ends Well*, should want Bertram after the way he has treated her, or why Hero, in *Much Ado*, should care to take Claudio back after the way he has acted, is difficult to understand; and Oliver's reformation and Duke Frederick's conversion in *As You Like It* are too sudden to be wholly convincing. However, we are probably not to take these matters too seriously, as witness Shakespeare's titles to the plays: *All's Well that Ends Well, Much Ado about Nothing, As You Like It*.

The suicide of Paula, at the end of *The Second Mrs. Tanqueray*, is somewhat forced, as though the playwright, after placing his characters in a difficult situation, did not know quite how to solve

* *A Note on Happy Endings,* in Volume III of the collected works of St. John Hankin. (London, Martin Secker, 1912).

the problem. The ending is one of the weaknesses in an excellent play, as Paula has not been presented as the kind of person who would kill herself. The marrying off of Mrs. Erlynne at the end of *Lady Windermere's Fan* seems rather a device to get rid of her than a logical happening. These endings are better, though, than the artificial ones of melodrama, where the hero is saved at the last minute by the arrival of the United States Army or the heroine is rescued in the nick of time by the faithful servant who happens to be passing by. Such artificial and providential intervention is known as the *deus ex machina* (derived from the Greek plays in which a god actually came down in a machine to solve human difficulties). In a well-thought-out and well-made play the ending, as has been said earlier, is implicit in the beginning, and there is no need for outside help to arrange matters.

THE THREE UNITIES

Along with the tradition that a play must have five acts is another, also borrowed from the Greeks, that a play must observe the three "unities" of time, place, and action. The classical French drama alone consistently observed the unities, which the Greeks themselves adhered to only generally. Originally the unity of time meant that the story of a play must not extend over a greater length of time than that necessary for the acting of it. The Greeks soon modified this principle to extend the limits to twenty-four hours. Most, but not all, Greek plays observe the unity of time. Strictly speaking, the unity is disregarded as soon as a play taking an hour or two to perform tells a story covering a period of twenty-four hours, and it is only a step further to tell a story covering several days, weeks, or years. The unity of place means the use of the same scene throughout; most Greek plays observe this unity, but there are a few exceptions. The unity of action, meaning restriction to a single plot, with no deviations or irrelevancies, was the one unity preserved strictly. Tragedy and comedy were never intermingled. The unity of action kept tragedy uncompromisingly serious and solemn; the so-called "comic relief," which later playwrights inserted in a serious play, was withheld by the Greeks until the tragedy was ended, and then supplied by the afterpiece.

The three unities are seldom present in any one play today, although many plays observe one or another of them. Modern plays range, as far as unity of time is concerned, from a story of a few hours to that of generations; as for unity of place, they may have one scene unchanged, or they may wander over the world; and for unity of action they may substitute many interwoven plots and frequent changes of mood. The playwright of today, whether he keeps to the classical unities or not, concerns himself with the unity of structure and design. The unities of time, place, and action are far from unimportant in modern drama, but they are secondary in the playwright's mind. First of all, the subject must assume the form best suited to it, and plays that would seem to lack unity in the older sense conform today to a larger unity of structure and design perhaps even more artistic because of its flexibility.

Chapter 5

TRAGEDY

THE THREE MAIN TYPES of drama are tragedy, comedy, and a combination of the two that may take the form of either serious-drama or comedy-drama. Tragedy has always ranked as one of the highest and most artistic works of civilized man. The greatest plays have been tragedies, although why they should be greater than comedies or other forms of drama has never been satisfactorily explained. Perhaps the frustrations, failures, and defeats of man bring out his nobler qualities in a way that his successes and triumphs seldom do. Perhaps human dignity appears to better advantage in sadness than in happiness.

The writer of tragedy treats of the serious side of life. His attitude may be kindly and tolerant, bitter and resentful, curious and questioning, or calm and resigned, but it is always sincere. He feels deeply about his subject, for he can not expect to move audiences unless he himself is moved. His seriousness, sincerity, and emotion are part of a conviction that man, no matter how noble and worthy he may be, is doomed to defeat in his aspirations hopes, and ambitions. Man may be the cause of his own downfall or it may come through some outside force, but in either event it is inevitable. The conflict in tragedy always ends disastrously for the protagonist, and in Greek and Elizabethan drama he always died. Modern drama recognizes that persons who endure great suffering may continue to live and be the victims of just as tragic a fate as death.

The effect of tragedy on the audience or reader has best been described by Aristotle, in the *Poetics*, in the well-known passages on arousing pity and fear for the fate of the hero, culminating in the catharsis, or purgation, of emotion. A great tragedy does not make us feel morbid or depressed; rather it uplifts us, "purifies" us, so that we feel better for having seen or read it. The story that has moved us may be far from our experience, but we feel akin to the hero as we watch his struggle against the forces that are inexorably destroying him. Our sympathy with him during his hours of trial not only broadens our understanding of human suffering, but leaves us chastened in spirit, sobered by the thought that tragedy is the lot of man, and that we ourselves may some day be the victims of a similar fate.

Tragedy presents the world as an imperfect place, where nobility of spirit and goodness of intention are often taken advantage of, where injustice is common, where unhappiness comes to those who deserve it least. The playwright, being an artist, creates a work of beauty as an expression of his thoughts, so that a tragedy is not only a moving story, but one expressed and presented artistically. A tragedy may be defined as *a play, written in a serious, sometimes impressive and elevated style, in which things go wrong and can not be set right except at great cost or sacrifice*. Things go wrong in life, but most of them are set right in time. In tragedy a great price must be paid before they are set right again. Sometimes the price may seem too great, as often in Shakespeare, but it is an axiom in the world of tragedy that the punishment is greater than the crime. Perhaps the keynote of all tragedy is expressed in Lear's, "I am a man more sinn'd against than sinning."

GREEK TRAGEDY

The first great drama in the western world was that of the Greeks. A knowledge of Greek drama is essential to anyone desiring a real understanding of modern drama, for the roots of our drama go back to the Greeks, who have furnished us with many dramatic principles and devices still in use. Greek tragedy, as it has come down to us in the plays of Aeschylus, Sophocles, and Euripides, is the starting place for any thorough study of the drama.

The form of a Greek tragedy was most important, as it was a

rigid one and every playwright conformed to it strictly. The out-standing characteristic was the presence of a Chorus, a group of persons who entered at the beginning of the play and stayed on the stage until the very end. The function of the Chorus was to announce the approach, entrance, and departure of a character, comment on what was being said and done, and philosophize about the characters in particular and life in general. The con-tinuous presence of the Chorus throughout the action of the play had an obvious effect on the kind of story that could be told. The principle of the unities came into being because of the Chorus; characters could not confide in one another or soliloquize while the Chorus was present, nor could they plan to do anything pri-vately or secretly. The Chorus, although it was a technical ad-vantage in some ways, limited the playwright considerably in his handling of plot.

The Greek dramatic formula consisted of ode and episode alter-nating, the ode being the song or chant of the Chorus and the episode being the speech of the actors. If the Chorus entered first, the play consisted of six odes and five episodes, as the Chorus was always the last to leave the stage. Sometimes the actors entered before the Chorus; the play then consisted of a prologue, six odes, and five episodes. The prologue was the one place where the characters could talk confidentially without being overheard by the Chorus, which had not yet entered, and the playwrights some-time took advantage of it absence. Thus, in *Antigone*, by Sophocles, it is in the prologue that Antigone tells her sister she is determined to see that their brother receives proper burial; once the Chorus of elders is present, any such plan of Antigone's would have been overheard and reported to the king, who had forbidden the burial. At the end of each episode the actors usually left the stage, which the Chorus then had to itself until the next episode. The five episodes are therefore loosely like modern acts, in that there is a complete break between each one and the one following; but as has been said before, they are more like scenes, since the presence of the Chorus means a continuous performance with no intermissions.

The number of actors in Greek classical tragedy never exceeded three. In early Greek tragedy, Thespis introduced the first actor, one member of the Chorus who stepped forward to address the audience and talk with the Chorus; Aeschylus added the second actor, Sophocles the third. The number of characters in a play could be greater than three, but there were never more than three speaking characters on the stage at a time. In other words, an actor might play several parts in the same play, but this was not difficult, as he wore a mask which he could change when he changed roles. As a rule the leading actor played only one part, that of the protagonist; the other two actors played the rest of the parts.

Greek plays were produced in huge outdoor amphitheaters, some of them seating as many as twenty or thirty thousand spectators. In such surroundings it was impossible for the actors to give individualized performances like those familiar to us today in our small, intimate theaters. In order to be seen properly by most of the audience, Greek actors made themselves larger by wearing thick-soled shoes (those worn by tragic actors were the buskin, by comedians the sock, hence the phrase "sock and buskin" for comedy and tragedy), padded shoulders, and a mask, which was a hollow figure of a human head made to match the rest of the costume in size. The masks were standardized and made according to type, so that the audience could tell at his first entrance whether an actor was a tragedian or comedian, hero or villain, king or peasant. It has also been suggested that the actor may have had some sort of voice amplifier inside the mask to make himself heard better.

The subject matter of Greek tragedy was known to most of the audience in advance, as originality of plot was considered less important than original treatment of well-known stories. The same plots were used again and again, if we may judge from the few plays that are extant. The murder of Agamemnon and the revenge and tribulations of his children, Orestes and Electra, was a favorite subject, treated by all three of the great writers of tragedy. (The Aeschylean trilogy is the basis of Eugene O'Neill's *Mourning Becomes Electra.**) One of the best known of the Greek

* See p. 85.

tragedies is *Oedipus the King*, by Sophocles, the famous story of
the man who killed his father and married his mother. The story is
continued in *Oedipus at Colonnus*, describing the death of Oedipus
as an old man, and in *Antigone*, telling the story of his daughters.
These family legends and stories of the past, which were the basis
of most Greek tragedy, may be compared with the stories of
persons like Queen Elizabeth, Mary Stuart, George Washington,
or Abraham Lincoln, which have been the basis of many modern
plays. An audience of today, seeing a play about one of these
persons, and knowing in general what it is going to be about, is
in exactly the same position as the Greek audience of classical
times.

Such a modern audience, seeing a play dealing with a subject
on which it already had a good deal of information, would be less
interested in the obvious and exciting dramatic situations that
could easily be included than in well-written and well-spoken
lines, careful and subtle characterizations, and a thoughtful understanding and interpretation of the problem involved. Partly because
the Greek audiences were already familiar with the materials,
partly because the Greeks were a highly civilized and well-estab-
lished people, and partly no doubt because of the presence of the
Chorus, Greek tragedy showed little or no violent action on the
stage. A necessary character in almost every play was a messenger,
whose duty it was to report to someone on the stage, perhaps the
Chorus, a battle, death, or any violent act that had taken place off
stage. The audience did not care to see the act itself; they were
interested in the effect of the act. Exciting incidents were not
lacking in the plays, but they took a subordinate place to a
philosophic belief, a pervasive atmosphere, that the actions of
man were governed by the Fates, and the main interest, therefore,
was in watching a man resign himself to them or be disposed of by
them.

This man, whom the Fates would strike down, was always a
person of note, of high station, and his fall was brought about because, as Artistotle said, of some fault or defect in his character,
or of some error of judgment. Thus the fall of a great man was
the usual theme of Greek tragedy. *Oedipus the King* does not

dwell on the murder of a man by his son and the son's subsequent marriage to his mother—these things had happened long before the time of the play. The audience is interested in the effect on Oedipus when he discovers what he has done. It is not a matter of punishment for a terrible crime, for Oedipus was not wilfully a criminal—the Fates had decreed the crime, and it had been prophesied that he would commit it; but what will happen to a great king who, through no fault of his own, is placed in a horrible predicament? Antigone, a princess, breaks the law by violating a decree of the king, but she does so to obey a higher law that is to her more important. Greek tragedy, because of its philosophic background, possesses an impressive and stately dignity unsurpassed in the history of drama.

In *Antigone*, retelling a well-known story, the playwright has made the conflict of universal interest by means of the larger implications underlying the problems of the two chief characters. The calm and dignified treatment of the plot exemplifies Matthew Arnold's description of Sophocles as one "who saw life steadily, and saw it whole." Antigone's attitude is one of quiet determination. There is no doubt in her mind that she will disobey Creon's decree, even though the penalty is death. She faces the dilemma of disobeying the king or of disregarding a religious obligation to bring peace to her brother's spirit. But the real issue, so far as she is concerned, is her own integrity—it would be noble to disobey Creon, base to obey:

I shall rest, a loved one with whom I have loved, sinless in my crime; for I owe a longer allegiance to the dead than to the living: in that world I shall abide for ever.

The conflict is between divine law and man-made law, and it is presented first from the point of view of Antigone.

But Creon has his point of view, that man-made law is necessary for the good of the state:

Never, by deed of mine, shall the wicked stand in honor before the just; but whoso hath good will to Thebes, he shall be honored of me, in his life and in his death.

Obedience to the state comes first. Toward his son, who begs him to listen to the voice of the people and honor, not punish Antigone for her deed, he is scornful:

CREON: Shall Thebes prescribe to me how I must rule?
HAEMON: See, there thou hast spoken like a youth indeed.
CREON: Am I to rule this land by other judgment than mine own?
HAEMON: That is no city which belongs to one man.
CREON: Is not the city held to be the ruler's?
HAEMON: Thou wouldst make a good monarch of a desert.

Creon is the absolute ruler, whose will alone decides what is good for the state.

When the two points of view clash, Creon is the apparent victor, for he imprisons Antigone and sentences her to death. But the victory is not a decisive one. Antigone is ready to die; she is glad she has broken Creon's law, and she will answer to the gods, not to him. His own son questions his authority, and the Chorus takes Antigone's part. Creon remains unmoved until the blind prophet warns him that the gods are displeased because he has disregarded them, and foretells death in his household as a punishment for his misdeeds. Troubled, he bows to the inevitable—"We must not wage a vain war with destiny"—and decides to free Antigone. His decision is the turning point of the play. The two points of view, divine and man-made law, have clashed in every episode; the most decisive clash causes Creon to change his mind. But we know he will be too late. Things have gone wrong, and they can not be set right. If the problem were as simple as that, if it could be solved so easily, it would not be a worthy subject for great tragedy. The conflict is between two irreconcilable ideas.

The Fates bring about Creon's downfall because he has defied the will of the gods. There is a similarity between his too late arrival at the cave and Friar Laurence's too late arrival at the tomb in *Romeo and Juliet*. Because of Antigone's death, Haemon kills himself, and because of his death, Eurydice, Creon's wife, kills herself. Creon's punishment is complete, and he prays for his own death as the Leader of the Chorus chants the closing lines:

Wisdom is the supreme part of happiness; and reverence towards the gods must be inviolate. Great words of prideful men are ever punished with great blows, and, in old age, teach the chastened to be wise.

The play thus ends on a quiet note—the final moment of serenity that succeeds the tragic tempest is particularly noticeable in Sophocles.

Modern drama shows many evidences of its Greek ancestry. Although the unities are not nowadays generally adhered to, whenever a play observes one or more of them it is following the Greek model. A play with few characters, especially one that has never more than three actors on the stage at once, is making use of the simple pattern of the Greeks. The Chorus is almost obsolete, although it reappears occasionally;* but the confidant, who knows the hero's inmost thoughts and serves as his adviser, the character who is clearly in the play as the author's mouthpiece, and the philosophizing character who utters wise sayings are its modern counterpart. The quiet, restrained play, often a one-act play, with singleness of plot and emphasis on effect rather than cause, where the personal fate of the characters seems bound up with the larger issues of life and death, is essentially Greek tragedy in modern dress.

SHAKESPEAREAN TRAGEDY

Shakespeare was England's greatest poet and the world's greatest playwright. By general agreement his plays are considered among the finest literary achievements of the human mind. No other writer of plays has written so many masterpieces or consistently maintained such a high level of beautiful poetry, and no other writer whatever has created such a distinguished group of memorable characters who utter so many quotable, and quoted, lines. Shakespeare is still the most popular playwright in our theater, and he is as alive today as when his plays were first produced. Each generation discovers him for itself; our grandparents went to see Ellen Terry, Henry Irving, Edwin Booth, Richard Mansfield,

* A striking modern use of the chorus is in Eliot's *Murder in the Cathedral;* the Stage Manager in Wilder's *Our Town* and Tom Wingfield in Williams' *The Glass Menagerie* are also modern examples of the Chorus.

and were thrilled by the fresh interpretations the actors gave to the famous roles; our parents have vivid memories of Sir Johnston Forbes-Robertson, Robert Mantell, E. H. Sothern, and Julia Marlowe; today we are thrilled anew by Katharine Cornell, John Gielgud, Maurice Evans, Orson Welles, and Laurence Olivier, who make the plays they appear in astonishingly ageless and vital. It is said that every actor has an ambition to act Hamlet, as every actress wishes to act Juliet; to the actors themselves these roles are apparently the supreme challenge of their art. No worthy production of Shakespeare has ever failed to attract large audiences, composed from his own day to the present, of persons from all classes of society.

It is not easy to reduce Shakespeare's ideas to a consistent philosophy, although some have tried to do so. He seldom commits himself as an individual. On the one hand, there is evidence that he accepted the Anglican view of divine providence, as expounded by Richard Hooker and other churchmen. Consider, for example, Hamlet's lines,

> There's a divinity that shapes our ends,
> Rough-hew them how we will,

or the words of Albany in *King Lear*:

> This shows you are above,
> You Justicers, that these our nether crimes
> So speedily can venge!

On the other hand, Gloucester, in the same play, directs our attention to a wholly different view of the world, which is not entirely dissipated by the outcome of the tragedy:

> As flies to wanton boys are we to the gods,
> They kill us for their sport.

Whether or not Shakespeare accepted the Anglican notion of divine providence, his theory of tragedy, at least in his greatest contributions to the *genre,* is that man brings about his own downfall because of some weakness of character. The Anglican notion of divine providence, be it noted, was that although God foresaw all things, he did not necessarily foreordain every occurrence. In Shakespeare man is brought low by a tragic flaw, inherently part of him, which he is powerless to overcome until it is too late.

Shakespeare's world is a just and moral one. If the punishment may seem too severe, especially that of the good characters, it is always at least to some extent justified. Lear's cry, "I am a man more sinn'd against than sinning," touches the heart, but the significant thought in the line is the acknowledgment of "sinning," the first time in the play that Lear has really called himself guilty. On the other hand, it is difficult to justify the deaths of such lovable characters as Cordelia and Desdemona. They did not deserve to die, but in tragedy things go wrong and can not be set right until the price is paid. If the price seems an unjust one, we feel with Othello "the pity of it." If it is in payment for a crime or wrong-doing, we are relieved and satisfied. Evil and evildoers are always punished in Shakespeare; no one may break the moral code without making restitution or paying the penalty.

Great tragic characters are not so much concerned with the world's justice and morality as they are with the higher morality within themselves. The greatest crime is being false to oneself, and the greatest triumph, which is often achieved only after much suffering and mental anguish, is finding one's true self. Death may come to the character soon after he finds himself, but he dies nobly and with dignity. We feel deeply moved, not with pity, but with respect and admiration. Hamlet can not understand his delay in avenging his father's murder:

> I do not know
> Why yet I live to say "This thing's to do;"
> Sith I have cause and will and strength and means
> To do't.

At the end of the play, when he finally kills the King, and is himself dying, his chief concern is that Horatio clear his name before the world:

> What a wounded name,
> Things standing thus unknown, shall live behind me!

The noble Brutus, who thought to help his country by killing Caesar and found himself merely one of a band of conspirators, can satisfy his conscience only by suicide, when he finally finds peace:

> Caesar, now be still:
> I kill'd not thee with half so good a will.

Othello, who had betrayed himself when he so basely misjudged Desdemona, makes no excuses for himself at the end and asks no mercy:

> Speak of me as I am; nothing extenuate.

Macbeth at the end of the play is weary of life, which had promised him so much and given so little:

> It is a tale
> Told by an idiot, full of sound and fury,
> Signifying nothing.

Lear's suffering is out of all proportion to his sins, but it brings about his regeneration and true sense of values. All he cares for at the end is the love of Cordelia, whose dead body he has just carried on the stage:

> This feather stirs; she lives! If it be so,
> It is a chance which does redeem all sorrows
> That ever I have felt.

It is passages like these that give us our finest moments in the theater, the catharsis, which lifts tragedy out of the realm of storytelling and makes of it a never to be forgotten experience.

Shakespeare's plays were produced on a platform stage that extended into the audience, which surrounded it on three sides. The outer stage was bare of scenery; the inner stage, which was a recess to the rear of the platform and separated from it by curtains that could be drawn, and which was used for bedrooms, studies, caves, tombs, and other interior scenes, could be furnished with such simple scenery as was necessary. Most of the acting was done on the outer stage, so that the actors were in the midst of their audiences instead of facing it as they do today. The theater

was a round or octagonal building open to the sky, so that the
groundlings, who stood in the "pit," were at the mercy of the
elements. The three tiers of galleries, which contained benches
for those able to pay for seats, as well as part of the stage, were
protected by a roof. The first public theater in England and the
model for all the others of the period was built by James Burbage,
the father of Shakespeare's leading actor Richard Burbage, and
the circular opening in the roof, the covered galleries, and the
platform stage were reminiscent of the inn-yard in which earlier
plays had been presented, with a platform in the middle of the
court, and the porches and balconies from which the spectators
could look down.

The Elizabethan theater, like the Greek, influenced the drama
of its time. The actors went in for declamation and oratory, and the
playwrights wrote them long speeches to show off their elocu-
tionary ability. The absence of scenery necessitated descriptive
passages explaining the locale; the lack of lighting effects called
for unusual art in depicting a night scene. On a bare stage, with
sunlight streaming in through the opening in the roof, the playwright had to convince the audience of *Macbeth* that the scene
was a heath, during a storm of thunder and lightning, or the audience of *Hamlet* that the watch was on guard on a platform before
the castle at midnight. The shape of the stage prohibited the
tableau, used so effectively in later theaters with curtains. The
Elizabethan stage had to be cleared at the end of every scene, and
if a character died on the stage, provision had to be made for
getting him off. There were intermissions between acts, but there
were none between scenes, the endings of which were usually
indicated by a rhyming couplet. The length of a performance is
told us in a line from the Prologue of *Romeo and Juliet*: "The two
hours' traffic of our stage." Even with no pauses between scenes
the plays must have been cut and the actors must have spoken
much more rapidly than they do today if the two-hour limit was
always observed. Although the outer stage had no scenery, the
actors wore elaborate and expensive costumes, not those of the
period of the play's action, but contemporary English clothes.
Producers who present Shakespeare in modern dress are doing

nothing new, as the plays were originally similarly presented. To-day they are generally given in period costume, as more befitting the language.

The tragedies of Shakespeare were not original in plot. Like the Greek tragic writers, he took familiar stories, shaping them to his own ends and for the actors in his own company—the originality lay in the treatment. His tragic heroes, already known to many of the audience through story, history, or earlier plays, took on new life and meaning by becoming living individuals facing problems related to everyday life, psychological studies with universal appeal. Perhaps Shakespeare's greatest contribution is his remarkable gallery of character portraits, many of which have taken their place in our lives as though they were actual persons. It is a fact that only a few persons in history have had as much written about them as has Hamlet, a creation of a playwright's imagination. The characters appear in plays that are a combination of great drama and great poetry, a combination rarely to be found outside Shakespeare.

In *Romeo and Juliet* the tragedy is brought about not through a tragic flaw in the protagonists, who are almost, if not quite flawless, but through fate, which is against the lovers from the beginning. That they should have to pay, with their lives, for the enmity between their families, makes them tragic figures, although not to the same extent as Shakespeare's later tragic characters, who cause their own downfall. Fate, as in a Greek tragedy, governs the action, but does not dominate it. The characters in Greek tragedy accept the decrees of fate with resignation: Romeo and Juliet, individualists where their love for each other is concerned, struggle against overwhelming odds for the right to be together. Romeo's "Then I defy you, stars!" when he learns of Juliet's supposed death, could never have been uttered by Antigone. Although fate has the final victory, the difference in attitude between the Greek and the Elizabethan outlook is unmistakable. In a Greek play the peace between the two families might have seemed worth the price paid, but Shakespeare makes us feel that the feud was senseless, and not worth such great sacrifice. Our sympathies are entirely with the lovers, who through no fault of their own loved, struggled, and died.

The chief conflict in *Romeo and Juliet* is the eternal one between youth and parental authority, treated from the standpoint of youth, as *King Lear* treats of the same conflict from the standpoint of old age. The feud of the Capulets and Montagues, which results so disastrously—two Capulets, two Montagues, and two relatives of the Prince die because of it—is the background of the plot, and gives occasion to most of the dramatic situations, but the lack of confidence and understanding between Juliet and her parents and Romeo and his is the real tragedy. The two lovers stand alone against the world, strong only in their love. It is because they are so alone, except for each other, that they have become the accepted models of what young lovers should be like.

The sense of swiftness, of a sudden, overwhelming love so intense that it destroys the lovers, is a Shakespearean touch not in the sources on which the play is based. The lightning strikes, and destruction follows. The entire action of the play is packed into less than four days. It is on a Sunday morning that the opening street fight occurs, it is that night the lovers first meet, and it is the next day that they are married. Although everything seems to be favoring the lovers, there is an underlying tragic motif, for Juliet wonders if their actions are not "too rash, too unadvised, too sudden," and the Friar warns, "They stumble that run fast." Then comes the fight with Tybalt, an hour after the marriage, and things begin to go wrong. Fate, which had been kind to them, now turns against them. Romeo's farewell to Juliet is early the following morning, and on that same night she takes the sleeping potion. Wednesday morning she is buried in the monument, later in the day Romeo is told the news, and in the early hours of Thursday he joins her in the tomb. The death of the lovers is the climax of the play. The element of accident, against which we were forewarned by the Prologue's mention of "star-cross'd lovers," is greater as the climax is approached than anywhere else in the play. It is an accident that Romeo arrives at the tomb just when Paris is there, thus adding another death to the total; had Romeo come a few minutes later, he would have discovered that Juliet was not really dead; had the Friar come a few moments earlier, or Juliet awakened sooner, Romeo's death would have been averted. But by now the crowding of accidents merely heightens the tragic effect; we know that fate has doomed the lovers, and that nothing can save them. Their death, however, is really a victory, for by dying they have shown the greatness of their love and may be said to have transcended every worldly obstacle.

King Lear, like *Romeo and Juliet*, treats of the conflict between youth and age, but it has a wider application and a deeper significance than the earlier tragedy. *Romeo and Juliet* is not a picture of the world, as *King Lear* is; one play tells the story of two star-crossed lovers; the other is a story of filial ingratitude, of children pitted against parents, of old age at the mercy of youth. In *King Lear* the conflict is not only between Lear and his daughters and Gloucester and his son, but between all parents and their ungrateful children. We are shocked at the depths to which human nature sinks in the play; we are horrified and dismayed at Shakespeare's implication that he is presenting common occurrences, a universal picture.

The general conflict in King Lear is twofold: between aged parents and ungrateful children, and between the good and evil forces in the world. The particular conflicts are many and varied. Two of Lear's daughters turn against him, he turns against the third daughter, and two evil sisters align themselves against the good one, and later against each other; Lear's conflicts are with his daughters and their husbands, with his loyal servant Kent, who tries to show him his error, with the Fool, who in a way represents Lear's conscience, with the storm, and finally with himself. In the sub-plot, Gloucester's evil son turns against him, Gloucester himself turns against his good son, and the two brothers are against each other. Gloucester, in the main plot, is loyal to Lear, and thus comes in conflict with the forces trying to destroy the king. Each of the chief characters, with the exception of Lear, is aligned with either the good or evil forces, and thus each takes a part in the general conflict between them. Lear is the object of contention between the two forces.

The germ of the whole play is in the first scene. The division of the kingdom, deliberately planned to safeguard Cordelia, becomes, through Lear's sudden outburst of temper, the source of the tragedy. Lear knows that Cordelia is loyal and true, and that Goneril and Regan are evil, yet in a moment of pique—"Better thou hadst not been born than not to have pleased me better"— he sows the seed of his own undoing and that of Cordelia. Arrogance, love of flattery, and a hasty temper are his tragic flaws. But the play is also the story of Lear's regeneration, of his gradual realization of his faults until, at the end, he has completely purged himself of them. Cordelia, who does not appear again until the fourth scene of the fourth act, but whose spirit is present throughout, is one of the most lovable of Shakespeare's heroines; yet her tactlessness and bluntness are tragic flaws for which she pays the penalty. Her disgust at her sisters' hypocrisy is commendable, but her way of showing it is not; she expects Lear to remember what her sisters are and not to be taken in by them, yet she forgets his weaknesses and makes no allowances for him. The conflict between Lear and Cordelia starts the play, and pervades the main plot; their reconciliation brightens the last two acts, as their final reunion is the climax.

Lear soon discovers the mistake he has made. By the end of the second act he knows that Goneril and Regan, having stripped him of everything, do not care what becomes of him. The conflict in his mind is a complex of clashing emotions—his wrath at the injustice he has suffered, his increasing awareness of his own folly, and his despair as he realizes that he is tottering toward madness. In the sub-plot Edmund is succeeding in his designs. The evil forces are in control; the good forces seem powerless and ineffectual, with the possible exception of Cordelia, whose promise of help is a ray of hope. The first two acts may be thought of as a sort of prelude to Act Three, the storm scenes. If *King Lear* were a musical composition, the storm scenes would correspond to the central melody around which the rest of the work is built; hints of the melody are heard at the end of Act Two, it comes to full expression in Act Three, there are variations of it in Act Four; the last act is a conclusion to the piece. The third act is truly magnificent, and represents Shakespeare at the height of his powers. Lear at the mercy of the storm he has really brought on himself is one of the memorable figures in drama.

There is something grand, almost titanic, in Lear's defiance of the elements, as though each of two adversaries were calling on the other to do his utmost. (Kent says it is the worst storm he has ever experienced, and Lear says, "Pour on; I will endure.") Lear seems to realize that there are other points of view than his own:

> I tax not you, you elements, with unkindness;
> I never gave you kingdom, call'd you children,
> You owe me no subscription.

And in the same speech, in almost the same words he had used in the preceding act, he shows again how he has changed from what he was in the first scene:

> Here I stand, your slave,
> A poor, infirm, weak, and despised old man,

but a moment later he is in a rage, calling the elements "servile ministers" that have joined his two "pernicious daughters" to do battle with him. His regeneration is under way, but it is not yet complete. Impressed with the power of the gods who can cause such a storm, he warns all sinners to take heed, and "cry these dreadful summoners grace." It is then that he says, for the first time classing himself with sinners, "I am a man more sinn'd against than sinning."

But it is not the physical storm that troubles him:

> The tempest in my mind
> Doth from my senses take all feeling else
> Save what beats there. Filial ingratitude!
> Is it not as this mouth should tear this hand
> For lifting food to 't?

The storm is thus symbolic of the conflict in his mind, an outward representation of his mental state. While he is still sane he utters his prayer, a touching speech that shows how unselfish he has become, one of the most beautiful passages in Shakespeare: "Poor naked wretches, wheresoe'er you are," who are in a storm like this, "How shall your houseless heads and unfed sides . . . defend you from seasons such as these?" His regeneration is almost complete. A moment later, with the entrance of "Poor Tom" Edgar, his overburdened mind gives way. What he has feared has come to pass, and weakened by suffering and exposure, he goes mad.

Lear's madness is the turning point of the play. Unlike most tragic heroes, who are actively concerned in the most decisive clash between the opposing forces, Lear is a character who is acted upon by the forces. In the first half of the play the evil forces become more and more powerful; they have reduced Lear from an imperious monarch whose word is law to a lonely and almost friendless madman, wandering about the heath in a storm. The good forces are negligible. When Lear loses his mind, it would seem that the evil forces have won, but now the good forces bestir themselves, they gradually become stronger while the evil forces grow weaker, until at the end the good forces are in control, although at a terrible cost.

Lear's regeneration is complete when he is reconciled with Cordelia, who has found him and placed him under a doctor's care. His mind restored after a soothing sleep, he kneels to beg her forgiveness:

> I am a very foolish fond old man,
> Fourscore and upward, not an hour more or less . . .
> If you have poison for me, I will drink it.
> I know you do not love me; for your sisters
> Have, as I remember, done me wrong:
> You have some cause, they have not.

This is not the king of the first scene, but an entirely new Lear, whom suffering has made over. He is humble and grateful for Cordelia's love:

> You must bear with me:
> Pray you now, forget and forgive: I am old and foolish.

Cordelia, overcome with pity and love, is concerned only for her father's comfort, and thinks not at all of his former injustice toward herself. In her loyalty and unselfishness she stands out among all Shakespeare's heroines; she is the embodiment of good, and a fitting leader of the good forces in the play.

At the end of the play, with the good forces in control, the entrance of Lear with the dead body of Cordelia in his arms is one of the most moving scenes in drama:

> A plague upon you, murderers, traitors all!
> I might have saved her; now she's gone for ever!

He lays her tenderly on the ground and speaks to her:

> Thou'lt come no more,
> Never, never, never, never, never!

Then he thinks that he sees her lips move, that she is alive, and in a moment of happiness he dies. This is the climax. Lear has suffered greatly, but his final moment is a happy one, though it is an illusion. We would not have him live; we feel with Kent,

> he hates him much
> That would upon the rack of this tough world
> Stretch him out longer.

That peace and order have again been established in Britain does not interest us greatly. One description of tragedy is that starting from a state of calm, it goes through storm, back again to calm. More than most plays does *King Lear* answer the description. But as in *Romeo and Juliet* our sympathies are not with the families whose feud is ended but with the lovers, so in *King Lear* our interest is in the story of King Lear—of his tragedy, his suffering, his regeneration. Our greatest interest is in Lear as a man, who only through suffering found the real meaning of love and human dignity.

It is right to think of Shakespeare as a world playwright, but we must not forget that he wrote for his own actors, his own audiences, his own time. Although the scene might be Denmark, Venice, Egypt, Rome, or Verona, the characters were typically English, speaking of contemporary matters in the idiomatic language of the day. The profundities and complexities of character were probably lost on the greater part of the contemporary audiences, who enjoyed the stories for their own sakes. The tragedies were

popular, but not for the same reasons as they are today. *Hamlet*
was an exciting revenge play, *Macbeth* a play about a murderer
who was finally punished, *Othello* about a man goaded into com-
mitting a murder by his "friend" who takes a fiendish delight in
torturing him. Elizabethan audiences enjoyed stories of hate,
murder, and revenge, and unlike the Greeks, who preferred violent
action off stage, wanted to see as much action on the stage as
possible, the bloodier the better. They were not insensible to love
stories, and they liked to hear poetry, especially long passages
that would seem out of place to most modern audiences, but most
of all they demanded action and excitement. Shakespeare was
wise enough to give them what they wanted, knowing that once he
caught their attention, he could hold it by giving them what *he*
wanted. His appeal was to everyone, as Ben Jonson realized when
he wrote the prophetic words,

<blockquote>He was not of an age, but for all time!</blockquote>

MODERN   TRAGEDY

Modern drama may be said to begin with Ibsen. In England,
where the drama had been dormant for almost a century (the
closet plays, as has already been explained, were a contribution
to literature, not to the stage), the so-called "renascence" began
with the translation of Ibsen's plays into English and their introduction to the English stage, and with the plays of Henry Arthur
Jones and Arthur Wing Pinero. Given this impetus, a new age of
drama, of which we are still a part, came into being in England
and America. If it does not possess the enduring grandeur of the
Greek or the robust vitality of the Elizabethan, modern drama yet
takes its place among the important periods of dramatic activity.
Notwithstanding the large number of mediocre and poor plays,
which make their appearance in almost every age, to be forgotten
by succeeding ages, modern drama is wonderfully rich in plays
dealing with the serious problems of the day, and in a variety of
form and expression that shows our playwrights eager to experiment and not accept completely the rules and conventions of the
past.

Ibsen's importance was in the form as well as the subject matter of drama. His contributions to the improvement of dramatic technique were the exclusion of the soliloquy and the aside (the soliloquy has returned, but in a more natural guise); the presentation of retrospect and other explanatory material simply, naturally, and especially economically; the linking of the past with the present, so that the retrospect is scattered through the play, not crowded in at the beginning and then dropped; the unaffected entrance on and exit from the stage of all the characters, instead of the obvious and often stilted movements in earlier plays; finally, and most significant, a meaty dialogue, full of suggestion, with overtones and undertones so pervasive that the most ordinary conversation may seem pregnant with meaning. As for subject matter, Ibsen created the drama of ideas, the play that was meant to be more than entertainment for the public—it was meant to stimulate thought and discussion. Whether they dealt with reform or with larger philosophical questions, the plays of Ibsen caused excited comment, showing that a playwright could arouse public interest just as effectively as an editor, an orator, or a statesman. Today the problems raised in many of these plays have either been solved or else have lost interest for us, but the plays still live as excellent examples of dramatic art.

Ibsen's early plays were romantic because of their idealized treatment of the past or their excursions into the domain of poetic fantasy. Among the historical plays are *The Vikings at Helgeland* and *The Pretenders*; the poetic fantasies are *Brand* and *Peer Gynt*. Next came the realistic plays, the social studies that revolutionized drama and were subjects of fierce controversey when they first appeared. These include *Pillars of Society, A Doll's House, Ghosts,* and *An Enemy of the People*. Then came the plays that were still realistic in technique, still interested in social problems, but with the attention centered more and more on psychological analysis —*The Wild Duck, Hedda Gabler,* and *Rosmersholm*. Last came the symbolic or mystical plays, which some find too difficult to understand, although others consider them among the best of Ibsen. *The Master Builder* and *When We Dead Awaken* are in this group. As a world playwright Ibsen belongs with the three great

writers of Greek tragedy, with Racine, Corneille, and Molière of
French drama, with the German Hauptmann, with Bernard Shaw
—only Shakespeare outranks them. As an influence on our drama of
today no one has been more important than Ibsen.

The modern tragic hero is no great man of eminence, fallen
from his high position. The playwright of today sees man as a
victim of his environment. It is not fate that defeats him, as in
Greek tragedy, or a tragic flaw, as in Shakespeare, although both
are often present. Man's enemies are his surroundings, either
those made by nature or those made by men, especially the codes
of laws, morals, and conventions that society has built up to
protect itself against those who, whether through strength or
weakness, refuse to conform to the general pattern. In *Ghosts*
Ibsen has tried to show that when society's code of morals becomes
outmoded, conformity is a weakness and may bring disaster. Mrs.
Alving has not the strength or the courage to break away from
conventions that she knows are false. "I am half inclined to think
we are all ghosts," she say in a significant passage. "It is not only
what we have inherited from our fathers and mothers that exists
again in us, but all sorts of old dead ideas and all kinds of old
dead beliefs and things of that kind." The one meaning of "ghosts,"
that they represent old, dead ideas and tyrannical conventions, is
the basis of Mrs. Alving's tragedy; the other, that they represent
hereditary traits that may warp the individual's life, provides the
story of Oswald.

Mrs. Alving is one of the great tragic heroines of drama. She
reminds us of Antigone; she is faced with a difficult choice, and
there is no way out for her. Antigone died with the satisfaction of
knowing she had done the right thing, but Mrs. Alving, at the end
of the play, is faced with either a living death or a remorseless
conscience. The finality at the end of *Antigone* and the prospect
of continued suffering at the end of *Ghosts* are characteristic of the
age each play represents. Mrs. Alving may also be compared with
Nora Helmer, for *Ghosts* and *A Doll's House* are companion plays.*

* For a discussion of *A Doll's House*, see pp. 135–137.

It was as if Ibsen, who had been severely criticized because Nora left her husband, had said, "All right, I'll show you a woman who did *not* leave her husband. She had as much, or more, reason to, but she stayed; I'll show you what happened to her." Another link between the two plays is that the congenital disease of which Doctor Rank is a victim, which is of minor importance in *A Doll's House*, becomes a major interest in *Ghosts*. When Nora discovered that her marriage rested on a false foundation, she faced the facts and courageously set out to find, by herself, her true place as an individual; when Mrs. Alving discovers that her marriage has become a farce, she has not the courage to defy conventions and face the facts, but continues to live a lie, with tragedy inevitably resulting. When Nora found that things had gone wrong, she at least tried to right them, at the sacrifice of her most precious possessions, her children; when things go wrong with Mrs. Alving, she prefers to do nothing rather than assert herself. The main conflict in *Ghosts* is Mrs. Alving's choice of disillusioning Oswald about his father, which would relieve his mind of his own responsibility in catching the disease, but might have other serious consequences, or of continuing as she has done and keeping the truth hidden. More horrible is her dilemma at the end, when she has to decide whether or not to administer the morphia tablets to Oswald.

Oswald's conflict is against the fate that has ruined his life— the syphilitic taint which is affecting his mind, which will eventually cause a permanent softening of the brain. Heredity, of which he is the victim, is one of the modern equivalents for the Greek conception of fate; there is no way of escaping it. For a time there is a glimmer of hope in Oswald's mind—he thinks that Regina may be his salvation, that with her strength and vitality his life might be bearable. But again heredity balks him: the sins of the father that are causing his mental breakdown have made Regina his half-sister. As an artist, he has keenly enjoyed the mere sensation of being alive, but sensation is now to be taken from him. He is not afraid to die; what he cannot face is the prospect of becoming an imbecile, of living on year after year without a mind.

Besides the similarity between Mrs. Alving and Antigone, *Ghosts* has many of the characteristics of Greek tragedy. It observes the unities of time and place, and its action of less than twenty-four hours is the culmination of a story that began thirty years earlier. Most of the play is talk—discussion and explanation—but the end of every act is a dramatic moment. There are few endings in modern drama to compare with the thrill and horror of the last scene of the play. As Oswald sits looking dully before him, with the blank expression of a man whose mind is gone, his mother must make her dreadful decision. If she keeps her promise to him, she will become the murderer of her son; if she does not, his life and hers will be a living death. Antigone made her choice, and was glad to die for what she knew was the right; Mrs. Alving's choice is not shown to us; Ibsen drops the curtain as she is trying to make it.* As Antigone is the victim of fate, Mrs. Alving is the victim of social convention. Antigone may seem the stronger character; yet Mrs. Alving suffered in silence many years for what she thought was best—her love for Oswald. That her sacrifice is in vain makes her all the more noble a figure. Her tragedy is as inevitable as Antigone's, for environment and heredity are merely new names for fate.

If man protests against the modern social order, and tries to fight for right and justic, as in *Winterset*, by Anderson, or in the tragedies of Odets, he is simply crushed. If he is bewildered and frightened by the world, and tries with a desperate helplessness to escape the deadly routine, like Mr. Zero in Elmer Rice's *Adding Machine*,† he is likewise crushed. If he tries to fight bigotry, false accusations, or in other words McCarthyism, as in Miller's *The Crucible*, the result is the same. Sometimes it is nature he is fighting, as in Synge's *Riders to the Sea*, where the villagers find in the sea, from which they are trying to make a living, almost a human antagonist; or in O'Neill's early plays, in which "that old devil sea" seems very much alive and terrifying. The tragedy of the common man of today may be just as impressive as the tragedy of a king or a prince

---

* When Nazimova played Mrs. Alving, she gave Oswald the morphia, on the ground that Ibsen wrote the last scene to be performed as the actress or director chose. In most productions the curtain falls with Mrs. Alving still irresolute.

† For a discussion of *The Adding Machine*, see pp. 146–148.

of the past; as far as modern tragedy is concerned, all men are created equal.

A good example of modern tragedy is *A Bill of Divorcement*, by Clemence Dane, which, like *Antigone* and *Ghosts*, poses a true dilemma from which there is no escape. A man is so badly shell-shocked in the war that his mind gives way, and he is placed in an insane asylum. His wife has remained faithful to him for a number of years, but at last falls in love with another man, plans to divorce her husband and remarry. At this juncture, entirely unexpectedly, the husband returns from the asylum, his mind recovered, eager to resume life where it had left off for him. It is a great shock to him to discover that his wife, having believed him permanently lost, sincerely loves another. He pleads with her for his right to happiness, which he had lost through no fault of his own; is he to be penalized for having gone away to fight for his country? But he also realizes her right to happiness; must she lose the love she has found after many years of loneliness? It is to the credit of the playwright that she does not compromise with the situation she has created, but allows it to lead logically to an unhappy ending. For whichever choice the husband makes, to refuse to divorce his wife, or to divorce her so she can marry the other man, someone is bound to be unhappy. It is the war that causes this tragedy, a series of circumstances set up by society; no one in particular is to blame, but things go wrong, and can not be put right at all.

The foremost playwright of America is Eugene O'Neill, who was awarded the Nobel prize for literature as well as three Pulitzer prizes, which are given annually for the "original American play performed in New York which shall best represent the educational value and power of the stage." Like most playwrights of distinction O'Neill was continually experimenting. His most effective experiments were the use of the monologue in *The Emperor Jones*, through which device most of the story is told, the use of the aside in *Strange Interlude*, by means of which he tells us what the character is thinking to himself as a complement to what he says aloud, and the modernization of a Greek trilogy in *Mourning Becomes Electra*, which is a New England version of the Agamemnon story.

His plays are in the main tragedies, although he also wrote serious drama and comedy.

O'Neill was concerned with the fundamental emotions and relationships of man, and he expressed them in stories that are forthright and simple—sometimes almost to the point of crudeness—but at the same time imaginative and soul-stirring. His characters are not ladies and gentlemen of the polished world; they seldom come from the high places. They speak their thoughts plainly, for though they may have poetry in their hearts, they do not use the heart's language. They are given to thinking about themselves, and some of them brood too much for their own good. One weakness of O'Neill as a playwright was that he presented as universal certain happenings that were distinctly limited in range, making generalizations about human nature from stories too localized to be representative. His outstanding quality is the fitness of his material for the stage; he was thoroughly at home in his medium, and his plays are good "theater" in the best sense of the word.

The Emperor Jones is a study of fear. Jones, Negro ex-Pullman porter, ex-convict, has made himself the absolute ruler of a tribe of West Indian Negroes whom he robs unmercifully, planning to decamp with his spoils when there is nothing left for him to take. When the natives rebel against his tyranny, he knows the time has come. He starts off jauntily enough, but as he loses his way in the jungle, his fears mount, his mind reverts to his past, then to the past of his race, until he has become like a primitive savage in both mind and body. The natives finally track him down and kill him, but his own fears, more than anything else, have conquered him. With the exception of the first and last scenes, the play is a monologue by Jones.

Beyond the Horizon, one of the earliest and best of O'Neill's plays, is the story of two brothers, one the dreamer, who wanted travel and romance, but who stayed on the farm to marry the girl he thought loved him, the other the materialist, who goes out into the world in his brother's place. Both are disillusioned in their search for happiness, and both are failures. *The Hairy Ape* is the story of a stoker on an ocean liner, who considers himself the most important person on the ship, the one who really makes it go; when a young society girl faints at the sight of him and calls him a "filthy beast," he realizes that he is not so important in the world, that there is a world outside the ship; he tries to enter that world, and finds that he does not belong; it comes to him that he does not belong anywhere, and finally in a zoo an ape breaks loose from its cage, crushes him to death. Man is not at home in the universe, O'Neill says, and only in death does he perhaps finally belong. *Desire Under the Elms* deals with elemental passions of a New England farm family. Every member of the family desires something: love, security, lust, money, the farm; no one really satisfies his desire. Life is not easy in O'Neill's world.

O'Neill's most impressive tragedy is *Mourning Becomes Electra*. Like its model, the Aeschylean trilogy of the *Agamemnon,* the *Choephori,* and the *Eumenides* (the one Greek trilogy extant), the play consists of three corresponding parts, *The Home-Coming, The Hunted,* and *The Haunted.* The story is substantially the same, the Greek characters having their modern counterparts, although the playwright has added a few characters, mainly for "comedy relief," which of course had no place in Greek tragedy. The modernization consists in transplanting the story to New England at the close of the Civil War, and making the characters twentieth-century persons who discuss and present psychological ideas of the nineteen thirties. The play is worth study either on its own account, as an example of the experimental trend in the modern theater, or as a Greek play in up-to-date dress.

None of O'Neill's plays is negligible. Among those not so far mentioned *In the Zone* is a series of one-act plays, powerfully presenting the ordinary seaman in his life at sea. *Marco Millions* is the story of Marco Polo and treats one of O'Neill's favorite themes—material versus spiritual values. *Ah, Wilderness!* is a pleasant comedy of adolescence, the one comedy amidst the serious plays and tragedies. *Lazarus Laughed* is based on the Biblical character; O'Neill thought this his best play. *The Iceman Cometh,* one of the most pessimistic of American plays, has been called O'Neill's version of *The Lower Depths;* it is a sort of American parallel to Gorki's play. *A Long Day's Journey Into Night* and *A Touch of the Poet,* both produced and published, at the playwright's request, not until after his death, are largely autobiographical.

O'Neill holds a secure place in American drama. He gave fresh life to the American theater, and was the inspiration of many younger writers. If he fell short of greatness, it was because he lacked the gift of high poetic expression called for by his characters and situations.

Classical and Elizabethan tragedy were written in verse; modern tragedy is largely prose, with some exceptions, although there are indications that the poetic tragedy may be once more becoming popular. Poetry and tragedy go naturally together. The belief that the public does not appreciate poetic plays is dispelled whenever a first-rate poet writes a first-rate play—as witness the striking success of T. S. Eliot's *Murder in the Cathedral*, and the work of Maxwell Anderson. The rarity of poetic drama today is not to be blamed on the audience, which does not care for indifferent drama even if the poetry is good, or good drama if the poetry is bad. When the exceptional combination of a great poet and a great playwright appears in our theater, he need not worry about his welcome.

Maxwell Anderson is second in importance only to Eugene O'Neill as America's foremost playwright. He may have lacked O'Neill's keen sense of theater, but he was endowed with a more facile power of expression, and he made a serious attempt to establish poetry as a natural medium for modern drama. He wrote a number of plays, in both prose and poetry, and won the Pulitzer prize once and the Critics award twice. His first popular success, written with Laurence Stallings, was *What Price Glory?*, a lusty and realistic comedy of World War I. His remaining plays were tragedies, serious dramas, and histories, most of them in verse.

Anderson's most important contribution to American drama was probably the poetic historical tragedy. Anderson, who wanted to do bigger things for the American stage than *What Price Glory?*, came to the conclusion that if the great tragic writers of the past always went to earlier ages for their stories, and always wrote them in verse, modern tragic writers must do the same. His first venture in this field was *Elizabeth the Queen*, which became a great success. Then came *Mary of Scotland, Valley Forge,* and *Anne of the*

Thousand Days, all of them impressive poetic historical tragedies. *Winterset,* a poetic tragedy based on a contemporary tragic theme (the Sacco-Vanzetti case), does not seem to have the lasting qualities of the historical plays.

Next to O'Neill and Anderson in importance as an American playwright, but perhaps destined to supplant them, is Arthur Miller. Certainly Miller is our foremost living American playwright. His interest in the drama has always been serious and he insists that the playwright not merely entertain but have something to say. This seriousness reflects the influence of Ibsen on his work, leading him to adapt *An Enemy of the People* for a successful Broadway production. "I have tried," he has said, "to take dramatic situations from life which involve real questions of right and wrong, and then find the moral dilemma and try to point a real, though hard, way out. A writer can't write anything decent without using the question of right and wrong as the basis." In discussing Aristotle's concept that the hero of tragedy must be a man of stature, Miller points out that times change and that "even a genius is limited by his time and the nature of his society." It does not matter whether the hero is a great man or a little man, whether he falls from a great height or a small one; what does matter, Miller says, is his intensity—he must have "fanatical insistence upon his self-conceived role." These two elements, the question of right and wrong, and the fanatical intensity, are present in all his plays.

Death of a Salesman, his best play, seems likely to become a classic. Many of those who see it speak of the "terrific impact" it makes on them. The reasons are many. Willy Loman (notice— *low man*) is an ordinary little man, like the rest of us, and we feel closer to him than to most dramatic heroes. He has taken a lifetime to pay for his home, now it's paid for, the children have left, and there is no one to live in it. He has bought a refrigerator on time, but before he owns it it has broken down. He thinks his two sons are the salt of the earth, but they are worthless shams, and deep down Willy knows. Parents want more for their children than they had themselves, and the children turn out badly. When this happens, parents blame the children, but if parents were really honest with themselves, they would put the blame on themselves. Willy knows where the fault lies, but he refuses to face the facts. He has his illusions. "A salesman is got to dream, boy," says Charlie at Willy's funeral at the end of the play. "It comes with the territory."

Willy lives in his dream world, but the world of reality is beginning to take its toll, and he is slowly losing his grip—and his mind. His wife Linda speaks for Miller when she tells the two boys, "I don't say he is a great man. Willy Loman never made a lot of money. His name was never in the paper. He's not the finest character that ever lived. *But he's a human being, and a terrible thing is happening to him.*" This last sentence could be a definition of modern, or any, tragedy.

In one of the most moving scenes in modern drama, Biff, who has come to terms with himself, tries to make Willy understand. Biff has always loved his father, but the memory of the woman in the Boston hotel room has stood between them; Willy knows that Biff holds this against him. Biff tells Willy off—if Biff is no good it is Willy's fault, but he doesn't hold it against Willy any longer; he just wants to be himself, and he wants Willy to give up his phony dream. He falls to his knees and holds on to Willy, who "fumbles for Biff's face." Willy's reaction to this outburst is the sudden realization that Biff loves him, and he stands there, in the playwright's words, "astonished, elevated." Willy and Biff have found each other again; Willy is back in his dream world. The real, though hard, way out for him is suicide, so that his sons may benefit by the insurance money. That the way out is real only for Willy, that the solution is not practical, that Biff and Happy will always be worthless, does not matter. Willy for a moment achieves a nobility that places him with other tragic heroes. In fact, earlier in the play Biff compares Willy to Hamlet. Willy's dream may be phony, but it is real for him. The intensity Miller speaks of is there. *Death of a Salesman* makes its appeal through commonplace characters, speaking commonplace language, living commonplace lives, but the tragic overtones lift the play to the realm of the universal.

Two of Miller's other plays worthy of mention are *All My Sons,* the story of a business man who made money unscrupulously for his family and then found himself facing the "moral dilemma"; and *The Crucible,* which tells about witch-hunting in Salem in 1692, but is really about McCarthyism. In the play the witch-hunting is carried on with a frenzy that is terrifying; lies are believed, the wildest accusations are accepted by those in authority, any attempt to present the truth or to try to show that the charges are fraudulent is rejected. This, Miller says, was McCarthyism.

Another major American playwright is Tennessee Williams, whose two early successes, *The Glass Menagerie* and *A Streetcar Named Desire*, are his best plays. They both deal with a favorite theme of Williams, the once proud genteel Southern lady gone to seed, the passing of the old aristocracy of manners and refinement. William's dialogue is realistic, almost brutally so in *Streetcar*, yet it contains another quality that causes one critic to refer to it as subjective realism. Williams and Arthur Miller are decidedly *American* playwrights in their thinking, much more so than O'Neill and Anderson, who deal with more universal themes.

Modern tragedy is not substantially too far removed from Greek or Elizabethan tragedy. If the protagonist is a little or a common man, the forces that he must fight and that eventually defeat him are usually overpowering. In modern tragedy man is the victim of the modern age.

Chapter 6

COMEDY

A SENSE OF HUMOR is one of the greatest assets of mankind, for it denotes not only cheerfulness and friendliness, but also lack of egotistical self-importance and pompous dignity. Comedy laughs at man, not at his misery or unhappiness, but at the things that can be genuinely funny—his mistakes, his follies, his minor misfortunes, his antics, his enjoyments. Comedy also laughs *with* man when he finds life happy and pleasurable. The main purpose of comedy is to create laughter, sometimes for its own sake, often for some ulterior motive of the playwright's.

The writer of comedy may treat of themes just as significant as those in tragedy, but instead of the serious he sees and stresses the humorous side of everything. His point of view is the opposite of the serious writer's, but he may have the same aim in mind—to tell a story that will make the audience think about some problem or state of affairs. Laughter, especially ridicule, is a potent weapon in the hands of a skillful writer, and may bring about change or reform more effectively than discussion or sermonizing. The comic writer's world is a laughable one; if the laughter is malicious or cruel, the world may seem to be turning bitter, but only temporarily. The conflict in comedy is a matter for laughter by the audience rather than concern, and if the protagonist is not always the victor (he usually is) the audience is always satisfied with the outcome.

The art of comedy is more difficult than the art of tragedy. Writers and actors know that it is easier to make an audience cry than to make it laugh, and many of them consider the creation of genuine laughter a greater triumph than the calling forth of tears. The effect of comedy is achieved in either or both of two ways:

through word or through situation. The comedy of word depends upon jokes, puns, witticisms, clever remarks about persons or things, brilliant repartee or dialogue. The comedy of situation depends upon characterization, and upon sets of circumstances created by the inventiveness of the playwright. The best comedies, of course, use both types to arouse laughter, the comedy of situation naturally giving rise to the comedy of word. Because meaning of words change as language develops, because topical allusions mean little to succeeding generations, and because styles of humor differ from one age to the next, comedies of the past are not so easy to appreciate as tragedies, especially if comedy of word overshadows comedy of situation. To the average audience or reader comedy is therefore more ephemeral than tragedy; a true appreciation of most comedy comes only with a knowledge and understanding of the age that produced it.

A comedy is a play written in a kindly or humorous, perhaps bitter or satiric vein, in which the problems or difficulties of the characters are resolved satisfactorily, if not for all the characters, at least from the point of view of the audience. Some of the characters may be left discomfited, or chagrined, or defeated, as in the plays of Ben Jonson, but on the whole the chief characters in comedy are left satisfied and happy, and we feel with them that all's well with the world and that it is good to be alive. The comic writer sees the world as a pleasant place in which to live; things may go wrong, but they are always set right before any great harm is done. Comedy exists not only to make us laugh, but to show us that human nature, with all its faults, is essentially good and deserving of happiness.

CLASSICAL COMEDY

As Greek tragedy contains the roots of modern tragedy, so Greek and Roman comedy are the forerunners of almost every type of modern comedy. Aristophanes wrote the best satirical comedy in the whole range of drama. Plautus and Terence created plots and characters that have been used over and over again by later playwrights. A knowledge of classical comedy is a great aid in the study of comedy through the ages, and well illustrates the saying, probably ancient when it was set down by the writer of *Ecclesiastes:* "There is nothing new under the sun."

Aristophanes, the greatest of the Greek comic writers and one of the greatest satirists in literature, wrote about fifty plays, the exact number being unknown. Eleven of them are extant; they are attacks on the Athenians of his day, individually and collectively, and are a sort of commentary on the life of Athens for a generation. *The Clouds*, one of Aristophanes' best, is an attack on philosophy, especially Socrates, who is taken as the type of the philosophical thinker of the time. *The Knights* is an attack on the demagogue, not only in general, but on one in particular. The *Wasps* is a satire on the Athenian love of lawsuits. *The Birds* is an allegory of a new and better Athens. *Lysistrata* is an attack on war. Since the men seem unable to put an end to war, the women of Athens band together to keep apart from the men until peace is declared. *The Frogs* is a literary satire. Aeschylus and Euripides contend in Hades for the throne of poetry, each reciting lines from his own plays to support his claim. Amusing in themselves, the comedies are valuable as revealing not only life in ancient Athens but the existence of a democracy that allowed free discussion of any person or subject chosen by the playwright.

The Old Greek comedies are divided roughly into three parts. First is a sort of general statement of the situation; then, somewhere about the middle, is the *parabasis*, a coming forward of the Chorus, which addresses the audience directly and gives the playwright's opinion of current topics and happenings; thirdly, the story is resumed in a loosely constructed series of farcical scenes. In conclusion there is usually a *comus*, or revel. The distinctive part of the play is the parabasis, in which the playwright could speak quite freely what was in his mind; apparently he often spoke too freely, for after a time the parabasis was prohibited by law.

The first part of *The Clouds* is a good-natured satire of Socrates and the "New Learning." The father who wishes to become a philosopher in order to learn how to avoid paying his debts is greatly in awe of Socrates and his Thinking Shop, especially when one of the disciples tells him how Socrates is occupied with such important thoughts as "How many times the length of its legs does a flea jump? and which end of its body does a gnat buzz through?" He is overcome when he sees the Master sitting in a basket suspended in the air, as befitting his superiority over ordinary men. Asked what he is doing up there, Socrates answers that he is traversing the air and contemplating the sun.

I have to suspend my brain and mingle the subtle essence of my mind with this air, which is of like nature, in order clearly to penetrate the things of heaven. I should have discovered nothing, had I remained on the ground to consider from below the things that are low; for the earth by its force attracts the sap of the mind to itself. It's just the same with the water-cress.

The source of the comic effect is the comparison of the philosopher with the man in the street, especially the latter's conception of the practical uses of philosophy.

After the parabasis, in which the playwright talks about the merits of his play, even though it did not win public approval by capturing the prize, and about various contemporary matters, we are shown some of the practical effects of philosophy. After Socrates has in disgust given up the attempt to teach the old man (his answers are really more sensible than the questions of Socrates, thus providing much humor as well as satire in the scene), the son agrees to be taught. He soon knows enough to beat his father, prove he is morally right in doing so, and says he will beat his mother too, because one ought to beat one's mother. The father, who has learned his lesson, calls a slave, and with his help burns down the Thinking Shop.

In Aristophanes the satire is almost savage in its attack on man's foibles and weaknesses. The attack on Socrates is much more than amusing—the philosopher, says the satirist, is corrupting the youth of Athens, and although the audience that first saw the play undoubtedly laughed at it, we should remember that Socrates was ultimately condemned to death on the charge.

The Clouds is a typical Old Greek comedy, but its appeal to us today, as in all great satire, is in the true picture it presents of human weakness. The conflicts of the play could easily be those of our own age—new ways of thinking as opposed to the old tried and true ways; the desire to obtain something for nothing by outwitting creditors; father and son trying to take advantage of each other for material gain; and right and justice eventually conquering evil and greed. We see ourselves as Aristophanes saw us.

The comedies of Plautus and Terence, the best of the Roman comic writers, deal with human nature in general rather than with specific persons or problems of the day. Many of their characters became types on the Roman stage, and some of them are still used by playwrights today. The braggart soldier, the miserly father, the spendthrift son, the parasitic friend, the family servant who pretends to be faithful to the father but is really partial to the son, the girl who marries against the wishes of her parents, or marries for love, not money, the shrewish wife—all these and others appeared in play after play, and were welcomed by Roman audiences as old friends. Later playwrights did not hesitate to take over these characters, and even the situations in which they were involved; human nature does not change much, and Plautus and Terence had hit on something fundamentally and eternally true.

The *Miles Gloriosus* of Plautus was the ancestor of many stories and plays about the braggart soldier. Nicholas Udall's *Ralph Roister Doister*, the first English comedy, is founded on it; Captain Bobadill, in Jonson's *Every Man in His Humour*, is a direct imitation of the character; Falstaff is a lineal descendant; Rostand's Cyrano is related, if not in the direct line; Bluntschli, in Shaw's *Arms and the Man*, is a variation; Captain Flagg and Sergeant Quirt in *What Price Glory?* are modern counterparts. Shakespeare's *Comedy of Errors* is based on the *Menaechmi* and the *Amphitruo*, and the later is of course the source of *Amphitryon 38*, by Jean Giraudoux, so named because it is the thirty-eighth retelling of the story. The *Aulularia* is the source of Molière's *L'Avare* and Shadwell's *Miser*. Of the plays of Terence, *Andria* is copied in Steele's *The Conscious Lovers*, and *Phormio* and the *Adelphoi* in Molière's *Les Fourberies de Scapin* and *L'École des Maris*.

The Miles Gloriosus, who is to swagger his way through many a later comedy, is a fool as well as a braggart, for he is easily imposed upon. He brags of his prowess to his parasite, who flatters him to his face and then in an aside calls him a boaster and a liar; the parasite does not mind flattering him as long as he supplies free meals as payment. His servant pokes fun at him behind his back because he thinks he is the hero of the city, when he really is the laughing-stock. The two lovers deceive him before his very eyes. He believes the courtesan who pretends to have divorced her elderly husband because she is in love with him. The credulous braggart is a subject for comedy on two counts—we like to see foolish credulity taken advantage of, and we enjoy seeing braggadocio deflated.

Although the braggart Captain and the two lovers are the chief characters in the story, the plot is really motivated by the actions of Palaestro, the Captain's servant, who is a master hand at intrigue. The intriguing servant is one of the most popular of the stock characters in classical comedy, and is to be found in every succeeding period of comedy. It is through Palaestro's scheming that the lovers are reunited; it is his idea to trick the braggart through the supposedly lovesick wife, really the courtesan hired for the purpose; and in the end, as a reward for his activity, he wins his freedom. The play depends on situations for its comic effect. The scenes in which the guard is hoodwinked into believing that there are two girls, twins, when it is the same girl, posing first as herself, then as her sister; the scene in which the Captain is flattered by Palaestro and the courtesan's maid, and struts about boasting of his accomplishments, not realizing that the two servants are having a good deal of fun at his expense; the departure of the lovers, the Captain eager to see his old love go that he may turn to his new love; and the entrance of the Captain into the house of the supposed new love, as the boy gleefully tells us that the trap is ready—such scenes are typical of intrigue comedy.

Roman comedy is less philosophical than Greek comedy, its characters are more standardized, and its action is swifter. The *Miles Gloriosus* is not so good a play as *The Clouds,* but its historic importance is greater, as the title character and the situations have been used again and again in later plays. The debt of modern comedy to classical comedy is incalculable, and is probably scarcely realized by many playwrights today. Whether we know it

or not, much of what we laugh at on the stage now was first thought
of some two thousand years ago in Greece and Rome.

SHAKESPEAREAN COMEDY

Shakespeare is not only our greatest writer of tragedy, but also
our greatest writer of comedy. Not the least remarkable of his
qualities is the ability to turn from one extreme to the other, which
he seems to do with the utmost ease. If his tragedies plumb the
depths of human experience, his comedies are a never-failing source
of delight to those familiar with them, a "brave new world" to those
who meet it for the first time, a happy place in which to relax and
smile and dream pleasant dreams. Shakespeare's comic world is
peopled with a wide variety of beings—fairies and spirits, lords and
ladies, country folk and city folk; sophisticated beings whose humor is intellectual, boisterous ones whose wit is rough and ready,
slow-witted ones who provide humor without knowing it; mis-
chievous pranksters, sighing lovers, amusing and philosophic
lookers-on at life. Some of them are sheer creatures of imagination,
fantastic and unreal; others are as human as ourselves, but idealized and romanticized for story purposes. In his comedies as well
as his tragedies Shakespeare is first and foremost a creator of
character.

Romantic comedy is the term usually given to the comedies, and
with a few exceptions it is an appropriate one, for most of Shakespeare's comic characters are romantic both in actions and in
words. Falstaff is like no other knight or soldier who ever lived.
Like his prototype, the Miles Gloriosus, he is a boaster, a liar, and a
coward; yet he is full of fun, a lovable character, and we would not
have him different. Bottom, the weaver, accepts his strange adventures in fairyland with the ease and self-assurance of a traveled
man of the world. And what are the rehearsing and presenting of
the play by the rude mechanicals but the spirit of romance! The
comedy of Rosalind breathes romance,* the battle of wits between

---

* It must not be forgotten that all feminine roles were taken by boys in
Shakespeare's time, so that there was an added element of comedy in seeing
a boy playing the part of a girl impersonating a boy impersonating a girl.

Beatrice and Benedick is a cloak that hides their real feelings for each other; Petruchio and Katharina are really in love. The comedies written in Shakespeare's last period, *Pericles, Cymbeline, The Winter's Tale*, and *The Tempest*, are almost pure romance.

But Shakespeare's comic world is not all romance and unalloyed happiness. There are serious moments in it, and serious characters who would seem to be more at home in another type of play. The Hero-Claudio plot in *Much Ado* belongs in a serious-drama, as does the story of the bond and the pound of flesh in *The Merchant of Venice. Measure for Measure* and *Troilus and Cressida*, sometimes referred to as Shakespeare's "bitter comedies," are really serious-dramas. Theseus, in *A Midsummer-Night's Dream*, is the matter-of-fact person to whom reason is supreme; poetry, joy, and romance to him are merely stories of the imagination:

> Such tricks hath strong imagination,
> That, if it would be apprehend some joy,
> It comprehends some bringer of that joy.

Yet he is not out of place in comedy, for at the end of the artisans' play he mentions "fairy time," he concedes that "this palpable-gross play hath well beguiled the heavy gait of night," and promises further celebration for a fortnight

> In nightly revels and new jollity.

The melancholy Jaques seems more like a companion to Hamlet than to the merry group in the forest of Arden, yet he too has his place in comedy—his melancholy is a "humor," a legitimate object of satire and laughter in the comedy of humors that Ben Jonson was making popular about the time *As You Like It* was written. Shakespearean comedy has its serious side, though it is made subordinate to gaiety and humor. Comedy to Shakespeare is something more than a means to arouse laughter—it is a philosophy of life.

Shakespeare did not restrict his comic characters to the comedies. If other playwrights before him mixed comedy with tragedy, none did so more adroitly or made the combination seem so natural. The comic scenes in the tragedies relieve the seriousness; but more important, they make the tragic scenes stand out all the more vividly by contrast. The grave-digging scene in *Hamlet* and the knocking at the gate in *Macbeth* are the best examples of the artistic use of comedy to heighten a tragic moment. Mercutio was so successful as a comic creation that he had to be removed in the middle of the play, before he overshadowed the hero, Romeo, in interest. And Falstaff, although the chief character in one comedy, *The Merry Wives of Windsor*, and at his best in the sub-plot of the histories, *Henry IV, Part I* and *Henry IV, Part II*, had also to be removed for perhaps the same reason—he had outlived his usefulness, and Shakespeare killed him off in *Henry V*.

In comedy as in tragedy Shakespeare was the practical man of the theater. He wrote parts for his comedians and was a master craftsman in the art of making audiences laugh. If some of the plays have a pair of comic characters, like Dogberry and Verges, the Nurse and Peter, and Launcelot Gobbo and Old Gobbo, the reason is that there were two comedians in the company for whom to provide parts. If the plays are crowded with puns, Shakespeare put them there because he knew the Elizabethan audience delighted in verbal play of any sort, especially puns. Notice the opening scene of *Romeo and Juliet,* between Sampson and Gregory, the Capulet servants, and watch how one comedian "feeds" lines to the other, in much the same manner that will be popular more than three and a half centuries later. Notice how Shakespeare takes the audience into his confidence when Prince Hal and Poins plan to rob the robbers and thus discomfit Falstaff, where a lesser playwright might have used the element of surprise on the audience as well as on Falstaff. Notice how the fun is sustained in scene after scene of *Taming of the Shrew*; or how individual comic scenes in *Twelfth Night* and *Much Ado* have a richness of humor all their own. Study the effect of the songs in the comedies. Shakespeare was a master of comedy as well as of tragedy because he knew how to attract and hold the attention of his audience.

As You Like It may serve as representative of Shakespearean comedy. A true romantic comedy, it has always been popular, largely because of its two principal characters, the enchanting Rosalind and the melancholy Jaques. The high spirits of Rosalind are as natural to her as the reflective attitude of Jaques is to him. More than any of Shakespeare's plays, *As You Like It* deals with the delights of the natural life—the quiet and happy atmosphere of the Forest of Arden is contrasted with the meanness and pettiness of the town and court. City life, as presented in the first act, versus country life, as presented in the second act, is a general conflict of the play.

> Blow, blow, thou winter wind,
> Thou art not so unkind
> As man's ingratitude.

The refining influence of the forest affects everyone for the better, even the two villains, who are suddenly converted and become extremely self-sacrificing. But the dramatic moments are less important than characterization, love scenes, presentation of pastoral life, songs, pleasing poetry, and delightful humor.

Rosalind's impersonating herself in order to give Orlando lessons in love is one of Shakespeare's happiest conceits. Romantic love, which was introduced to the English stage in *Romeo and Juliet*, and which became such an important element in the theater, was no part of classical drama. We have only to compare the love interest in the *Miles Gloriosus*—the Captain's affair with the girl and his proposed affair with the young wife, and the affair of the two lovers—with the love story in *As You Like It* to see what romantic love has added to the drama. The romance of Rosalind and Orlando would have been impossible in Greek or Roman drama; just as impossible would be *As You Like It* without their romance. The scene in which Orlando makes jesting love to a boy who he thinks is also pretending, but who really is in deadly earnest, is romantic comedy at its best.

The spirit of the pastoral scenes is suggested by Charles the wrestler, speaking of the banished duke in the forest, "and a many merry men with him; and they there live like the old Robin Hood of England." The duke himself strikes a deeper, truer note in his first speech—now that they have become accustomed to their new life, is it not "more sweet than that of painted pomp?" are not the woods "More free from peril than the envious court?"

> And this our life exempt from public haunt
> Finds tongues in trees, books in the running brooks,
> Sermons in stones and good in everything.
> I would not change it.

It is an ideal life, and amidst its peaceful surroundings many of the difficulties of the characters are solved. The only discordant voice is that of Jaques, who is most himself when "thus most invectively he pierceth through the body of the country, city, court." But he is always worth listening to. As the duke says,

> I love to cope him in these sullen fits,
> For then he's full of matter.

Jaques knows that the idyllic existence cannot be permanent, and that they must soon leave the forest to play other parts elsewhere:

> All the world's a stage,
> And all the men and women merely players:
> They have their exits and their entrances;
> And one man in his time plays many parts . . .

At the end of the play, the forest is left to those who belong there; the duke, although he "would not change it," gives up the quiet life to take his crown again, and the others accompany him to resume their normal lives. Duke Frederick remains to follow the religious life, and Jaques elects to join him: "out of these convertites there is much matter to be heard and learn'd." Perhaps Jaques makes the wiser choice in not returning to the court. The Robin Hood days have also left their mark on him.

But *As You Like It* is mainly a love story. The pastoral setting and the philosophical Jaques enrich the background against which the various lovers are revealed. It is only natural that the woods should be full of verses about Rosalind—

> From the east to western Ind,
> No jewel is like Rosalind . . .

for she dominates the play and motivates much of its action. The true love of Rosalind and Orlando, the devotion of Silvius, the scorn of Phebe, changing to infatuation for Rosalind, the affection of Touchstone for Audrey, and finally the love of Oliver for Celia, are evidences of the new romantic element that has come to the drama. *As You Like It* reveals Shakespeare in a kindly and friendly mood, showing us that romantic love is important in the world. In tragedy love may cause suffering and unhappiness, but in comedy it causes enjoyment and laughter, and a warm feeling around the heart that life is good.

COMEDY OF HUMORS

The comedy of humors, contrary to general belief, was not a creation of Ben Jonson, whose achievement was rather to make popular what had long been known on the stage. The two earliest English comedies, *Ralph Roister Doister*, by Nicholas Udall, and *Gammer Gurton's Needle*, by William Stevenson, are comedies of humor. Jonson added his own particular gifts to an older idea of comedy, and the combination started a new fashion in plays.

To understand the comedy of humors we must remember the physiological belief in Elizabethan times that the body contained four cardinal fluids or humors—blood, phlegm, bile or choler, and black bile. The normal man had these humors in correct proportion. When Mark Antony says of Brutus

> the elements
> So mix'd in him that Nature might stand up
> And say to all the world, 'This was a man!'

the meaning is that the four humors were so well fused that Brutus was a perfect man. An over-abundance of any one humor caused an abnormal condition. Thus an oversupply of blood (*sanguis*) made a man sanguine, too much phlegm made him phlegmatic, too much choler made him choleric, and too much black choler made him melancholy. The word *humors* was first the name of the fluids, then of the conditions they brought about; a man was said to be in a sanguine or phlegmatic humor, or his humor was put down as choleric, or melancholy. Soon the term came to mean any eccentricity, whim, or fancy thought to be caused by the faulty proportion of the fluids, and it is this use of the word that is meant by the comedy of humors. The chief character, representative of a type, was a person with a humor—he might be miserly, cowardly, misogynic, boastful, misanthropic (usually the humor chosen was one that made him unpleasant and irritating to others)—which was the basis of the plot. *The Humorous Lieutenant*, by Beaumont and Fletcher, for instance, does not refer to a witty lieutenant, although he causes much laughter in the play, but to a lieutenant with a humor, which happens to be that of boasting. Like Shakespeare's theory of tragedy based on the tragic flaw, the theory of the comedy of humors springs from the idea that a defect of character is innate in man.

Ben Jonson was the greatest of Shakespeare's playwriting contemporaries. One of the most scholarly men of his time, he wrote tragedies, masques, for which the celebrated architect Inigo Jones designed the stage settings,* and comedies, which are the most important of his works. His comedies are the opposite of romantic—they are intensely realistic, dealing with the common people, usually satirically, and relating them to the follies of contemporary London. By adding realism to exaggerated humors and writing in a satirical vein, Jonson brought a new type of comedy to the English stage. *Every Man in His Humour* was the first of the type, and tradition says that Shakespeare's efforts obtained it a hearing after it had been rejected as being too radical a departure from the comedy of the time. The new play was a great success, and the comedy of humors became definitely established. *Every Man Out of His Humour* was Jonson's next comedy; among his others, the best are *Volpone, or the Fox*, which has been revived on the modern stage and has been made into several modern motion pictures, *Epicoene, or the Silent Woman, The Alchemist*, which Coleridge thought was one of the three most perfect plots ever planned,† and *Bartholomew Fair*.

Every Man in His Humour displays all the main types of Jonson's humor characters, and also illustrates his use of humors to motivate

---

* A masque was an elaborate entertainment consisting of poetry, music, and dance, usually written for and performed by amateurs. The best and best-known masque in English is Milton's *Comus*.

† The other two were *Oedipus*, by Sophocles, and *Tom Jones*, by Fielding.

the action. Bobadill (taken directly from the *Miles Gloriosus*), Matthew, and Stephen are the would-be wits, the pretenders to gentility, who are clearly satirized and condemned; Knowell and Wellbred are the truewits,* and the real thing the would-bes are trying to imitate; Kitely is possessed of the humor of jealousy, exposed as a vice; the elder Knowell, the doting father with the humor of being too curious about the goings-on of his son, Downright, Cob, and Cash are almost farcical characters; last is Justice Clement, the completely whimsical or eccentric character, queer but likable. More than half the play is taken up with scenes of ethical or social satire, which do little to advance the plot, but serve principally to reveal the various humors of the characters.

The plot, based on the humors, shows Kitely, insanely jealous of his young wife, suspecting the visitors who come to his house, and even his wife, of tricking him. The would-bes get into trouble trying to imitate the truewits, and the truewits enjoy themselves at the expense of the would-bes. The elder Knowell seeks his son at Cob's house, whither Kitely's wife comes to seek her husband, and Kitely to seek his wife. In the general confusion that follows Kitely thinks the elderly man is his wife's lover, she distrusts her husband, Cob beats his wife for entertaining men, and Knowell promises to have them all arrested. Brainworm, in his various designs to help his master, young Knowell, is reminiscent of Palaestro, his predecessor in the *Miles Gloriosus*, and like him is responsible for many of the complications of the story.

In comparing Jonson's comedies with Shakespeare's, two fundamental differences may be noted: Jonson's characters are realistic, although they may be exaggerated for satirical purposes, whereas Shakespeare's, with some exceptions, are in the main romantic; and Jonson's technique follows classical rules, with which Shakespeare has little concern. Bobadill, the blustering captain, who is a great fighter until he has to fight, when he turns out to be a coward; Stephen, the country gull trying to act the man of the world; and Matthew, whose father was an honest fishmonger, and who is now, according to Cob, lowering himself by chasing after gentlemen, are undoubtedly true London types of

* Truewit is the name of a character in Jonson's *Epicoene*.

the day, as are the two gentlemen of fashion, Knowell and Well-bred. They and the other characters, whether farcical or not, might have stepped directly from the street to the stage. The characters in *As You Like It*, on the other hand, are to a greater extent the product of imagination. The characters of both plays are true to life, but on different planes. In structure, also, the two plays differ, one following the panoramic pattern of the Elizabethans, the other adhering more closely to the integrated pattern of intrigue characteristic of Roman comedy. The slow-moving first part of *Every Man in His Humour*, in which the emphasis is on character, and the rapid action in the fourth act, after the plot finally gets under way, are very reminiscent of Roman comedy; especially are the doings of Brainworm in the classical tradition.

Jonson's purpose in writing *Every Man in His Humour* was not merely to give a new type of play to the stage. As he tells in the prologue—his favorite medium for the formulation of critical theory—he intends to present deeds and language that "men do use" in everyday life, and characters that "show an image of the times." Follies of the day are to be laughed at as they deserve. Above all, human nature is presented as it is. The comedy of humors, as developed by Jonson, was soon a fixture in English drama. Other playwrights, including Shakespeare, created "humorous" characters, and Jonson was generally acknowledged to be the leader of the new school. Almost a century later a playwright of the Restoration period, Shadwell, imitated him slavishly, worshiping him as one "who was incomparably the best Dramatick Poet that ever was, or, I believe, ever will be." Today the comedy of humors as a type has almost disappeared; characters with humors, however, are still popular, mainly in secondary or subordinate roles.

COMEDY OF MANNERS

The comedy of manners was the most distinctive drama of the Restoration age. With the return of the monarchy and the reopening of the public theaters in London, the pendulum swung away from the gloomy seriousness of the Puritans, who had been a dominating influence for many years. The serious plays of the period presented an exaggerated idea of love, valor, and honor (they were called heroic plays or "love and honor" plays), as a sort of antidote to a lack of heroism in real life. The comedy of the period accepted man for what he was, and held the mirror relentlessly up to nature. Aristotle had said that tragedy represents men better, comedy worse than they really are. The Restoration comedy of manners contained characters unrivaled for their ready wit and clever repartee—and for their utter selfishness and heartlessness. Written for and directed toward a small, select audience (unlike Elizabethan plays, which appealed to all classes of society, Restoration plays were enjoyed only by members and satellites of the King's court), this comedy was less a reflection of the life of the times than of the inner group that constituted the fashionable society of the city of London.

Although the return of Charles II, after a long stay in France, signalized the importation of French ideas, many of them incorporated in the drama of the times, the comedy of manners was a native growth, a logical development from earlier English comedy. Jonson's satire on social affectation, especially his use of would-be wits like Matthew, Stephen, and Bobadill, and in contrast with them, true men of fashion like Edward Knowell and Wellbred, directly anticipates one phase of the comedy of manners. The other main phase, the usual theme of the plays, sex conflict, has its roots in such plays as Shakespeare's *Much Ado about Nothing* and the works of Beaumont and Fletcher. The Restoration did not create a new comedy, but rather adopted the comedy of a generation before to its own current needs.

The characters typified in the comedy of manners portray not only the "acquired follies" of mankind, as they were called at the time, but also the manners and conventions of the polite world of which both they and the audience were a part. Life to this group was a social function, a garden party. There were serious matters in the world, to be sure, but a man was invariably self-possessed, and did not speak of them in good society. To make a good appearance was of main importance. Love and sex are the central themes of the plays, and they were treated humorously in a way to displease and even disgust many who could see no good in them and no reason for their existence. No study or discussion of the plays can avoid the question of their immorality, which undoubtedly played a large part in their popularity. Our reaction to the conversation of these elegant ladies and gentlemen to whom courtly trifling was the chief business of life depends on our outlook. We may be practical and literal, as Macaulay was, or we may interpret romantically, as Lamb did.* The sensible attitude to take is to try to understand the times. The stress is not on the morality, but on the wit. Flirtation was an art that almost everybody felt obliged to practice; it was the fashionable thing to do, and one could not afford to lag behind. The plays depict

realistically and in a sinister spirit the life of the most dissolute portion of the fashionable society of the city. The hero is ordinarily a man pursuing the pleasures of drink, play, and love, with a complete disregard for the well being of others; and the heroine is a woman whose scruples, if she has any, are based on prudence rather than virtue. Great emphasis is laid on repartee for its own sake, and upon epigrams propounding an elaborate and systematic code of immorality.†

Witty, gay, artificial, heartless, immoral, disturbing, and yet delightful, the comedy of manners is what its name suggests—comedy to be enjoyed and laughed at, manners to be appreciated and understood.

Of the five chief writers of the Restoration comedy of manners, Congreve belongs at the top. *The Way of the World* is one of the finest comedies in English. The perfect example of the comedy of manners, it has never been surpassed in the polish and brilliance of its language. It is pure comedy, with underlying moments of seriousness, as in the proviso scene between Millamant and Mirabell, a high point in all comic writing. The way of Congreve's world is sometimes serious, although it may be cloaked in flippancy and

* See Macaulay's *Comic Dramatists of the Restoration,* and Lamb's *On the Artificial Comedy of the Last Century.*

† Joseph Wood Krutch, *Comedy and Conscience after the Restoration,* Rev. ed. (New York, Columbia University Press), p. 6.

wit. In the dedication the playwright says that he scarcely hoped the play would succeed on the stage (it was a failure when first produced), "for but little of it was prepared for that general taste which seems now to be predominant in the palates of our audience." The most polished example of the comedy of manners needs an audience of highest intelligence to appreciate it fully. The involved situations and intricacy of plot may be weaknesses, but those who are willing to grapple with these obstacles find themselves richly rewarded.

The relationship between the type characters of the comedy of manners and the comedy of humors may be seen in Mirabell, the truewit, and Witwoud and Petulant, the would-bes. Mirabell is the fashionable gallant, the witty man about town, the generous lover; but although a truewit, he is not above deceit and trickery to maintain his position. It is he who brings about a happy ending to the complications of the plot, in a *deus ex machina* manner, causing the discomfiture of the villains and gaining the gratitude of those he frees from persecution; yet he has made love to Lady Wishfort because he wanted to be near Millamant, her niece, he has been a lover to Lady Wishfort's daughter, and he has planned to trap Lady Wishfort, in order to humiliate her, into a marriage with his servant, disguised as a wealthy country gentleman. Witwoud and Petulant are witless fools, favorite characters in Restoration comedy. Petulant, to make an impression when he is in company, hires persons to call for him and pretend he is wanted; Witwoud, when his country brother comes to town on a visit, joins in the fun made of the stranger, who does not recognize the dandified fop as his brother. Scenes like that of the conflict of wits between the country squire and the coxcombs are the mainstay of the comedy of manners.

But our principal interest in the play is Millamant. Until her entrance, in the middle of the second act, the playwright does little more than mark time while he gives us in great detail the situation from which the comedy and the plot will develop. Her entrance is the real beginning of the action; we have been told a good deal about her, and we are not disappointed, as she is well worth waiting for. Mirabell describes her coming: "Here she comes, i' faith, full sail, with her fan spread and her streamers out, and a shoal of fools for tenders." She enters like a breath of fresh air, and we are immediately in the realm of witty repartee, of high comedy. In the intellectual give and take that follows between Millamant and Mirabell, we can see, underneath the raillery, that she really cares for him, as he does for her. But it is not the way of their world to say so openly, at least for a time. The first meeting of the two reveals the conflicts we are to expect—between Mirabell and Lady Wishfort; between those who would like to see Millamant and Mirabell married and those who would not; but the most distinctive conflict, characteristic of the age and its chief contribution to comedy, is that between the sexes, the light-hearted, sophisticated battle of wits between the two lovers. As far as the plot is concerned, the conflicts in the play are those often used before in comedy, but overshadowing them in interest is the intellectual conflict of the sexes, which in the Restoration has become a main preoccupation of comic writers. The most sprightly meeting of the lovers culminates in the well-known proviso scene, in which they lay down the conditions under which they will marry. The scene is the peak of Restoration high comedy, representing the sex conflict at its best. What should be noticed and remembered, however, is the seriousness underlying the wit, the deep attachment between the two, and especially, in an age when almost every subject was discussed frivolously in the world of fashion, a sincere and healthy respect for the marriage bond. Restoration writers often laughed at marriage, when it called forth laughter, but they admitted no impediments to the marriage of true minds.

The perfection of *The Way of the World* lies in its brilliant dialogue and characterization, and the consistency of the comic spirit. Good things are said not only by the leading characters, but by the minor ones as well—Congreve gives lines to his secondary characters that other playwrights would save for protagonists. The consistent high level of wit, which tends to artificiality at times, is the result of a purity of style that makes us ignore the unpleasantness (there is no grossness). Congreve's world is an idealized one, a world apart, created for the enjoyment of those who are at home among ladies and gentlemen of fashion, either real or imaginary.

Next in importance to Congreve is Wycherley. His two best plays are *The Country Wife*, which has been revived several times in recent years, and *The Plain-Dealer*, a transplanting to English soil of Molière's *Misanthrope*—both Wycherley's Manly and Molière's Alceste having been suggested by a French nobleman whom both playwrights knew. *The Plain-Dealer* is one of the most savage satirical plays ever written, a comedy of manners that bitterly attacks what other playwrights were content to treat merely lightly or jestingly.

Jean-Baptiste Poquelin, or Molière, was probably the most famous of all French playwrights and is considered by some to be the finest of all writers of comedy. Poking fun at pretense, hypocrisy, affectation, miserliness, snobbery, quackery, pedantry, his plays still give pleasure today because these qualities are universal and are always the legitimate butt of ridicule. *Les Précieuses Ridicules* pokes fun at affectation, *L'École des Maris* and *L'École des Femmes* at marital relations, *Tartuffe* is an attack on hypocrisy, *Le Misanthrope* on plain speaking, *Le Médecin Malgré Lui* on quackery, and so on. In *Amphitryon* and *L'Avare*, which is a caricature of miserliness, he went back to Plautus for his plots. One of his best remembered plays is *Le Bourgeois Gentilhomme*, with the delightful Monsieur Jourdain, who discovers he has been talking prose all his life.

Etherege, who wrote one of the first Restoration comedies of manners, was the author of three plays, the best of which is *The Man of Mode, or Sir Fopling Flutter*. One of the finest examples of the comedy of manners, it contains, in the character of Sir Fopling Flutter, perhaps the most famous of a long line of stage fops or dandies that has continued unbroken to the present. With his affected manner and talk, his dandified clothes, his witlessness, boring subjects of conversation, and silly self-importance, the fop has been the butt of jokes and actions ever since Etherege introduced him to English comedy. Vanbrugh, who was a well-known architect as well as a playwright, lacks the keen wit of Congreve or Etherege, and the biting satire of Wycherley, but he is full of fun and frolic. The line of descent of English comedy comes down through him. His best plays are *The Relapse,* a sequel to Colley Cibber's *Love's Last Shift,* and *The Provok'd Wife.* Vanbrugh's greatest contribution to the theater is Lord Foppington, in *The Relapse.* The epitome of foppishness, he has been called by Hazlitt "the personification of the foppery and folly of dress and appearance in full feather," and by Leigh Hunt "the quintessence of nullification." But he is not so silly as he seems, and knows every minute what he is doing. Vanbrugh's common sense endows even foppishness with some practicality. Farquhar, the last of the five chief writers of Restoration comedy, was too romantic (he was an Irishman) to write a true comedy of manners, and yet too much of a follower of the others to write a true sentimental comedy. His best play, *The Beaux' Stratagem,* is the last comedy of manners of the period and one of the early sentimental dramas, although not a pure specimen of either type. Full of freshness and breeziness, Farquhar added a healthy naturalness to what had been artificial comedy.

The comedy of manners was the basis of much of the comedy that was to follow in succeeding periods. Sheridan, in a sentimental age, followed in the footsteps of Congreve; Oscar Wilde, at the end of the nineteenth century, contributed his share to the renascence of English drama by writing comedies that likewise were in the Congreve tradition; today Noel Coward, S. N. Behrman, and Somerset Maugham are our best exemplars of the tradition, although many other playwrights are finding the comedy of manners the best medium in which to express themselves.

SENTIMENTAL COMEDY

The comedy of manners, because of its wit, its immorality, and its snobbish appeal to the few, was an obvious target for criticism and attack. The most telling blow was struck by Jeremy Collier, a non-juring clergyman, who in 1698 published his *Short View of the Immorality and Profaneness of the English Stage,* which started a heated and widespread controversy. Collier's attack did not kill the comedy of manners, but it brought about a serious set-

back, and paved the way for the comedy of sentiment, or sentimental comedy, the characteristic comedy of the eighteenth century.

The comedy that lent impetus to this *genre* toward the close
of the seventeeth century was written by Colley Cibber, actor,
playwright, theater manager, and poet laureate, who in his first
play, *Love's Last Shift*, presented something that seemed new
when, in a typical comedy of manners, he changed the ending so
that the rake reformed and was reconciled with his wife. The un-
expected reconciliation was a welcome alternative to the monot-
onous plots of the period, but it was not well motivated; the reformation of the hero is a little difficult to accept, and it is to be
feared that Cibber was more concerned with a dramatic novelty
than with a real change of heart in his character. Vanbrugh believed
so little in it that he immediately wrote *The Relapse* to show what
happened after the reconciliation; Cibber was delighted with the
new play and made perhaps his greatest success in the role of Lord
Foppington, his own Sir Novelty Fashion, in *Love's Last Shift*,
now raised to the peerage. Lord Foppington appears once more
in Cibber's *Careless Husband*, another sentimental comedy. When
Cibber saw which way the wind was blowing, that sentiment was
coming in, he worked the strain for all it was worth.

It was Sir Richard Steele, co-author with Addison of the *Spectator*, who established the sentimental comedy, expressing with
conviction and sincerity ideas that Cibber was probably only ex-
ploiting. Steele's essays and plays are filled with sentiment, in the
better sense (as opposed to sentimentality, which soon came in,
to become an ever increasing element in the literature of the age);
we find the idea of poetical justice now a prominent part of comedy,
and characters rewarded materially for their virtue and goodness.
From one of Steele's essays we have this description of a woman:
"Though her mien carries much more invitation than command,
to behold her is an immediate check to loose behaviour, and to
love her is a liberal education." The attitude toward women has
changed from that of the previous age—in fact, the entire attitude
toward life has changed, and as Hazlitt said of Steele's plays:
"It is almost a misnomer to call them comedies; they are really

homilies in dialogue." *The Conscious Lovers,* his best play, is a
typical comedy of sentiment; the lovers are sentimental, the play
attacks dueling, cold-blooded marriage contracts, and pride of
family, and the whole aim, of course, is to reform society.

As the century progressed, sentimental comedy became more
sentimental, more didactic, with more and more reflective sentences
put into the mouths of characters who were more and more genteel
and further and further removed from real life in their actions
and speech. "Genteel comedy" became a synonym for sentimental
comedy, and the main purpose of comedy, to arouse laughter, was
almost forgotten. *False Delicacy,* by Hugh Kelly, is a good example
of sentimental comedy. It was first performed six days before the
appearance on the stage of Goldsmith's *The Good-Natured Man;*
that it was a popular success where his own play was a failure
soured Goldsmith on sentimental or "genteel" comedy, and so in
She Stoops to Conquer he makes ironic allusions to gentility in
comedy. Although the plays of Goldsmith and Sheridan are
superior to those of the sentimental writers, the latter are not to be
dismissed lightly, their plays were a distinct contribution to the
time, and have much to recommend them.

In *False Delicacy* most of the characters are so afraid of hurting
the feelings of others that they are prepared to sacrifice their own
happiness rather than speak the simple truth that it would be to
everyone's advantage to hear. Lord Winworth confides to his
cousin, Charles Sidney, that his long devotion to Lady Betty has
ended in her refusal of him; Sidney thinks that Lady Betty really
has an affection for Lord Winworth, but has too much delicacy
to say so. Lord Winworth, however, has decided to pay his attentions to Miss Marchmont, a protege and companion to Lady Betty;
but Miss Marchmont, "being unhappily circumstanced with regard to fortune," and possessing "an uncommon share of delicacy,"
may "possibly think herself insulted by the offer of a rejected heart,"
and therefore, to save her embarrassment, he is going to ask Lady
Betty to speak to her for him. Sidney, who is engaged to Miss
Rivers but is really in love with Miss Marchmont, has too much
delicacy, of course, to tell Lord Winworth the truth: "Little does

he know how passionately I admire the very woman to whom he is immediately going with an offer of his person and fortune. The marriage with Miss Rivers, I see, is unavoidable; and I am almost pleased that I never obtained any encouragement from Miss Marchmont, as I should now be reduced to the painful alternative of giving up my own hopes, or of opposing the happiness of a friend." The sentiment and the language may sound stilted (they are strangely like those to be met later in the melodrama of the nineteenth and early twentieth centuries), but they were natural enough to the polished age to which they were addressed.

Lady Betty, of course, has cared for Lord Winworth all along, and realizes it fully only after he stops paying her attentions. Disguising her real feelings, she dutifully speaks to Miss Marchmont in his behalf, is gratified at the girl's refusal, yet secretly hurt that she must wound him by another refusal. Miss Marchmont, who really loves Sidney but whose delicacy prevents her from telling Lady Betty so, thinks she has hurt Lady Betty's feelings, and rather than offend her, decides to marry a man she does not love. And so it goes. Mrs. Harley, one of the few sensible characters, laughs at delicacy: "Well, thank heaven, my sentiments are not sufficiently refined to make me unhappy," which is as good a statement as any of the theme of the play. The general conflict, as we discover early, deals with "delicacy" and the complications it causes; the particular conflicts concern the various mismated lovers and their attempts to remain loyal to their sentiments as well as to their loves. If we are at all experienced in the ways of sentimental comedy, we know that in the end each lover will win the lady of his choice, and that each lady also will gain her heart's desire.

The play is a comedy of sentiment, but it is also a satire on the comedy of sentiment. Delicacy is all very well in its way, but false delicacy is another matter. It is the sensible persons who finally straighten matters out for the sentimental ones, who have "too much sense [sensibility] to be wise, and too much delicacy to be happy." The play ends on a true moral note. Lord Winworth says, "The stage should be a school of morality," and the last speech tells us that "the principal moral to be drawn from the transactions of today is, that those who generously labor for the happiness of others, will, sooner or later, arrive at happiness themselves."

The revolt against sentiment, instituted by Goldsmith, Sheridan, and other playwrights, although it brought true comedy back to the English stage for a time, did little to check the sentimental movement. Goldsmith expressed his feelings in several essays, one of them called *On Laughing and Sentimental Comedy*, in which he described the differences between the two kinds of comedy, and showed constructively what could be done in his two plays *The Good-Natured Man* and *She Stoops to Conquer.*

She Stoops to Conquer, or The Mistakes of a Night, is one of the most enduring of English comedies. Because it has been a frequent presentation by high school and college dramatic groups there is a tendency to regard it with some condescension. Actually it is a very wholesome comedy, and its laughable complications never fail to amuse. Young Marlow, timid and bashful before ladies of his own station, quite the bold ladies' man with girls who are inferior socially to him, Tony Lumpkin, the country bumpkin (why else such a name for him?), Mr. Hardcastle, who prefers the old-fashioned ways, Kate Hardcastle, who follows the modern ways in the daytime and the old in the evening, all contribute to the fun. The central idea, that a young traveler could mistake a large rambling house for an inn, was suggested to Goldsmith by an actual experience in his youth.

Sheridan, one of the most gifted of our writers of high comedy, and influenced most by Congreve, wrote three masterpieces of comedy: *The Rivals*, which consists of two plots, the comic and the sentimental, the comic of course being the more important; *The Critic*, a play about plays; and *The School for Scandal*, his best play and one of the great comedies of all drama. Its satire, straight from Molière, on the gossiping ladies of the fashionable world; the two brothers, Joseph Surface, hypocritical, holier-than-thou, thoroughly detestable, and Charles, extravagant, irresponsible, thoroughly likable; Lady Teazle (notice the name), flirtatious, exuberant, and her elderly husband; these are some of the elements that are compounded to make the play. Its famous screen scene, in which the various plots are brought together most skillfully is, like the proviso scene in *The Way of the World*, one of the high points in dramatic writing. *The School for Scandal* was the best effort of the anti-sentimental movement; after Sheridan there was little comedy for more than a century. Sentimentalism, which was a forerunner of romance, characteristic of the nineteenth century, never really died, and today the comedy of sentiment, modified somewhat, is firmly entrenched on our stage.

MODERN COMEDY

The renascence of the English drama, as has already been said, began with the plays of Ibsen, Jones, and Pinero. Ibsen, although he wrote a few comedies, was chiefly concerned with tragedy; Jones and Pinero wrote tragedy, serious-drama, and comedy, and their influence on comedy was marked. Such plays as *The Liars*, by Jones, and *The Gay Lord Quex*, by Pinero, gave English comedy well-written and well-constructed works, "social comedies" dealing with problems of the upper brackets of society, for other playwrights to follow.

More distinctive as an influence were the plays of William Schwenk Gilbert and Oscar Wilde. Gilbert, with his collaborator Sir Arthur Sullivan, brought new life and vigor to comedy with the series of delightful operettas that are as fresh and familiar to us today as they were to those who saw the original productions. Nonsensical, ridiculous, with a sort of systematic and logical absurdity, they are keen satires on English life, public and private; nothing is sacred to Gilbert, who attacks the high and the low alike, but always in the spirit of high comedy. Like other satirists he feels that the follies and traditions he is ridiculing need amendment; unlike most satirists, he is always in good humor, his weapons of attack are laughter and song, and if he is malicious at times, he is wittily so, and leaves no hard feelings behind. In Gilbert the comedy of manners is clothed in a fresh kind of wit, embellished with humorous ditties and "patter" songs on the one hand, and on the other with a romantic love story, which may have its ridiculous side, but which is in the true sentimental vein.

Oscar Wilde comes straight down from Congreve. *Lady Windermere's Fan* and *The Importance of Being Earnest*, his two best plays, are the representative comedies of manners of their time. With their sparkling dialogue, their clever and witty characters from the fashionable world, and their glittering epigrams, they are only a step removed from the height of pure comedy of *The Way of the World*, but their underlying interest in the social problems of the day reflects the nineteenth-century attitude toward life rather than that of the seventeenth century. Wilde's plays are better constructed than Congreve's. Notice, in *Lady Windermere's Fan*, the masterly handling of situation that results, at the end, in the even balance between Lord and Lady Windermere—he has a secret concerning her that he will keep from her, she has one concerning him that she will keep from him, and Mrs. Erlynne is the connecting link. Wilde not only caught the spirit of the comedy of manners, but was in addition an excellent craftsman of the theater.

The greatest name in modern comedy is George Bernard Shaw. Author, critic (in his younger days he was a music critic before he became a dramatic critic), playwright, novelist, essayist, satirist, Nobel prize winner, he was an outstanding figure in the world, and like all really important writers he had a wider audience than the immediate literary circle to which he made his first appeal. He was a critic of modern life, severe but constructive; if he tore down some of our cherished ideas, he showed us how to build them up again. Where other playwrights developed characters or situations, Shaw played with ideas—he was preeminently the playwright of ideas. Most plays are built on the formula of exposition, development, denouement or conclusion; Shaw, who was one of the first to recognize Ibsen's genius, said that Ibsen's formula was exposition, situation, discussion, and Shaw took over this formula. He wrote more than forty plays, most of them comedies, but he also wrote serious plays like *Heartbreak House, Back to Methuselah,* and the tragedy *Saint Joan.*

Candida, one of the most popular and most often acted of his plays, is a domestic triangle story discussing marriage. *Caesar and Cleopatra*, a modernization of the old story, gives Shaw the opportunity to discuss conquest and rule by military might; *Arms and the Man* is less philosophical and more of a spoof of the military, and was the basis of Oscar Straus' comic opera *The Chocolate Soldier*. *Pygmalion*, in which the Galatea is not a statue but a little cockney girl who is made into a lady, becomes a discussion of the English caste system and the various levels of society; it was the first of Shaw's plays to be made into a motion picture and is of course the original of the tremendously successful *My Fair Lady*. *Man and Superman* discusses the relations between the sexes; *Major Barbara* discusses poverty and wealth; *The Doctor's Dilemma* discusses medicine and doctors; *Fanny's First Play* discusses playwriting and critics. Shaw's Prefaces to his plays are full of meaty reading and give a clue to what is to be discussed in the plays they preface.

Shaw was a humorist of the first order. He created witty lines and funny situations, and was fond of writing with his tongue in his cheek, so that it is difficult to be sure, at times, when he was serious and when he was not. Stimulating, full of ideas, Shaw's plays are permanent contributions that entertain us and at the same time make us think—the argumentative playwright provides argumentative characters whose arguments continue long after the play has been seen or read.

James M. Barrie has used sentiment quite freely and openly as the mainstay in most of his plays. The combination of sentiment, solid themes, a delightful sense of humor, and a quality that is best described by the overworked word "whimsical" has produced plays of enduring charm and popularity. Among his best comedies are *The Admirable Crichton*, a delightful satire on class distinctions, and *What Every Woman Knows*, a humorous yet keen study of marriage.

Noel Coward has brought the comedy of manners up to date. His plays have the same emphasis on repartee for its own sake, the same interest in the situation of the moment rather than plot or character development, as do those of Congreve or Etherege. A true man of the theater, he writes plays, some of them with music which he himself composes; produces, directs, and acts;

and he can sing and dance as well as play "straight" roles. His attitude toward the drama, well expressed in the introduction to *Play Parade*, a collection of seven of his plays, is that of an enthusiastic craftsman who takes a keen delight in practicing his craft. His best comedies are *Design for Living, Private Lives, Hay Fever,* and *Blithe Spirit*.

In spirit a comedy of manners, its social significance somewhat dubious because the chief characters seem morally confused and because the playwright offers not a criticism of life to think about but a philosophy of life to laugh at, *Design for Living* is representative of the best of modern comedy. If, more than the other comedies examined in this chapter, it laughs at life itself rather than at the mistakes and follies of man, that is the privilege of the writer of comedy, and is as good a way as any of viewing life in this modern age. "I never intended for a moment," says Mr. Coward in the introduction to *Play Parade*, "that the design for living suggested in the play should apply to anyone outside its three principal characters, Gilda, Otto, and Leo. These glib, overarticulate, and amoral creatures force their lives into fantastic shapes and problems because they cannot help themselves." The playwright makes no case for any design of living; he simply created three characters (to fit the Lunts and himself, as he tells in the introduction) who, once they came to life, quite naturally muddled into their own design (although it took them three and a half years—the length of time covered in the play—before they stopped quarreling and accepted it).

As in the Restoration comedy of manners from which it is a direct descendant, *Design for Living* has a double source of enjoyment for the audience—witty dialogue and the conflict between the sexes. The intimate story of the three protagonists and their relations with one another forms the basis of the conflict, which varies each time the playwright manipulates the characters into a new situation. The general conflict between conventionality, represented by Ernest, and unconventionality, represented by Gilda, Otto, and Leo, is the background for the particular conflict that seems never-ending among the three principals. In the first act of the play the conflict is between Gilda and Leo, on the one hand, and Otto, who is furious because the two have betrayed him. He will not listen to reason: that they probably feel worse about it than he does, that it was unpremeditated and temporary, that Leo didn't take on so when Gilda chose Otto in the beginning. Otto leaves them, and in the second act we see Gilda and Leo together. Leo has become too popular and fashionable for Gilda's peace of mind, and the conflict is at the stage of Gilda versus Leo. When Otto returns, during Leo's absence, the conflict is at first between Gilda and Otto; then it is Gilda and Otto versus Leo; then, as Gilda runs away the next morning and leaves them both, it is Gilda versus Otto and Leo. In the last act Gilda, now married to Ernest, seems satisfied with her life, and the stage of the conflict is still Gilda versus Otto and Leo. But when the two come to visit her, she soon realizes that her happiness is bound up with theirs, and the three are bound together again: Gilda, Otto, and Leo versus the world.

The spirit of comedy is high throughout the play, as though the three were ever keeping in mind the dictum that life is too serious to be taken seriously, a point once made by Oscar Wilde. Ernest, who is the defensive force throughout the play, is faced with something he cannot understand, and he lacks the sense of humor to see the comedy of the situation—in the first act Otto returns to find Leo in his bed, in the second act Leo returns to find Otto in his, and in the last act Ernest returns to find the two of them in *his*. At the end of the play Ernest, angry and disgusted, stamps out of the room in a rage; as he leaves he falls over a package of canvases, a mishap which sets Gilda, Otto, and Leo off in a gale of laughter. Their laughter becomes uncontrollable as the curtain falls.

The laughter that climaxes the play is their answer to the world. Mr. Coward, to quote the introduction once more, says they were laughing at themselves. Whatever the reason for it, the laughter is the key to the understanding of the comedy. Like its Restoration forbears, *Design for Living* treats the sex conflict as a legitimate object of comedy, quite apart from any moral interpretation, which for the time being must be put aside. Gilda and Otto and Leo are laughing at themselves because they are having a good time, because they are indifferent to the rest of the world, which they hope will mind its own business as they are minding theirs and because it is good to be alive.

Among the noteworthy American comedies, three have already been mentioned: O'Neill's *Ah, Wilderness!*, the nostalgic story of adolescence at the beginning of the century, Anderson and Stallings' rowdy play of American Marines in World War I *What Price Glory?*, and Heggen and Logan's *Mister Roberts*, the World War II navy play, which, although it has a serious ending, is written in the true comic spirit. Others are *You Can't Take it With You*, *Of Thee I Sing*, *Dinner at Eight*, *Once in a Lifetime*, and *The Man Who Came to Dinner*, by Kaufman, *Biography* and *No Time for Comedy*, by Behrman, *The Animal Kingdom* and *The Philadelphia Story*, by Barry, *Life with Father*, by Lindsay and Crouse, *Bell, Book and Candle*, by Van Druten, *The Moon is Blue*, by Herbert and the delightful *Teahouse of the August Moon*, Patrick's adaptation of the Sneider novel.

It is in the field of musical comedy, however, that America has made a real contribution to the drama. *Oklahoma!*, the Rodgers and Hammerstein musical version of Riggs' *Green Grow the Lilacs*, was an innovation—instead of a haphazard story to fill the gaps between individual songs and dances, it had a story to tell, and the songs were an integral part of the story. Other Rodgers and Hammerstein plays were *Carousel*, based on Molnar's *Liliom*, *The King and I*, from Margaret Landon's *Anna and the King of Siam*, and *South Pacific*, based on stories by Mitchener. The plays are really comedy-dramas with appropriate music and lyrics; therein lies the originality. The lyrics of Oscar Hammerstein II are models of compactness, are often meaty with ideas, and are worth reading in their own right. Hammerstein's death was a grievous loss to American drama.

As modern tragedy is not far removed from older tragedy, modern comedy also shows its relationship to the past. Few human beings can resist laughing at others or themselves when laughter is called for. The chief function of true comedy, said Meredith, is to arouse thoughtful laughter, but whether thoughtful or otherwise, laughter in these troubled times will always have a place in the world.

Chapter 7

SERIOUS-DRAMA, COMEDY-DRAMA, AND OTHER TYPES

BETWEEN TRAGEDY AND COMEDY is a middle ground. Many plays are serious without being tragedy, or humorous without being comedy. The serious play that is not a tragedy may be called a serious-drama, examples of which are Henry Arthur Jones's *Mrs. Dane's Defence*, R. C. Sherriff's *Journey's End*, Sutton Vane's *Outward Bound*, John Balderston's *Berkeley Square*, Sidney Kingsley's *Men in White* and *Darkness at Noon* (from Koestler's novel), Ketti Frings's dramatization of Wolfe's *Look Homeward, Angel*, *The Heiress*, by Ruth and Augustus Goetz from James's *Washington Square*, Herman Wouk's *Caine Mutiny Court-Martial*, Lawrence and Lee's *Inherit the Wind*, Lillian Hellman's *Watch on the Rhine* and *The Little Foxes*, Marc Connelly's *The Green Pastures*, William Inge's *Come Back, Little Sheba*, Thornton Wilder's *Our Town* and *The Skin of Our Teeth*, Archibald MacLeish's *J. B.* These plays and many others obviously belong to a type of their own, and their large number forms an important body of drama.

Beaumont and Fletcher, contemporaries of Shakespeare and after his retirement the most popular playwrights of the Elizabethan stage, are usually given the credit for originating the type of play that is neither tragedy nor comedy but partakes of the attributes of each. They called this new kind of play "tragi-comedy"*—it contained no deaths of protagonists, therefore it was no tragedy, yet "brings some near it, which is enough to make it no comedy." The tragi-comedy became very popular, and

---

* The term was first used by Sir Philip Sidney in his *Apology for Poetry*, 1595.

Shakespeare himself, in his last few plays, followed the lead of his young friends. *Pericles, Cymbeline,* and *The Winter's Tale,* although classed as comedies and called romances, are really tragicomedies; but earlier Shakespeare, as has been mentioned, had written serious-dramas—*The Merchant of Venice, Measure for Measure,* and *Troilus and Cressida.* Whether Shakespeare, in his serious comedies, or Beaumont and Fletcher, in their tragicomedies or romances, first brought the serious-drama to the English stage, it has become increasingly important from their time to the present.

The writer of serious-drama treats of the serious side of life, but unlike the writer of tragedy he does not believe that man is always doomed to defeat. He sees life in terms of stirring emotions, exciting episodes, or significant experiences that deeply affect his characters without destroying them. Whereas the world of tragedy is an imperfect one, in which things go wrong and are set right only after a great catastrophe or sacrifice, and the comic world is a happy place in the main, where things may go wrong in order to make us laugh, but are set right before anyone is badly hurt, the world of serious drama lies between the two, a serious place where man gets into trouble, but also a pleasant place where his troubles disappear when he has learned his lesson. *A serious-drama is a play with the sincerity and earnestness of tragedy without its inevitability of impending disaster, and with the kindly and tolerant attitude of comedy without its underlying spirit of humor.* The conflict may or may not result in defeat for the protagonist, the ending may or may not be a happy one, but serious-drama always deeply moves us. If the catharsis be not so powerful as that caused by tragedy, it is because the inevitability of tragedy strikes at our innermost feelings. The writer of serious-drama may not be so great as the writer of tragedy, but he is often closer to the public, which probably finds his outlook on life more like its own and therefore more appealing than that of his sterner brother playwright.

Characteristic of most serious-dramas are tense situations, moments in which the conflict between the opposing forces is brought vividly to a head. These dramatic situations, in a tragedy, are usually subordinated to the theme of the play; although they are important, they are part of a more significant whole. In a serious-drama the dramatic situations are important in their own right, are often the reason for the play's being, and stand out by themselves as the very core of the play. *Mrs. Dane's Defence*, one of the best plays of Henry Arthur Jones, is the story of Mrs. Dane's attempt to keep her past from becoming known to the young man she is engaged to marry, and to his family. The big moment of the play is her cross-examination by the young man's foster father, who is a famous barrister, Sir Daniel Carteret. In one of the memorable scenes of modern drama, Sir Daniel questions Mrs. Dane about herself, is just about convinced that she is what she seems and worthy of being welcomed into the family, when a slip of the tongue on Mrs. Dane's part, a slight mistake of a single word, arouses all his suspicions as a lawyer, and he skillfully and mercilessly keeps at her until he has dragged out the truth. We remember the scene long after we have forgotten what the rest of the play is about; in a greater play such a scene would exist for the play's sake, but here the play exists for the sake of the scene.

In *Rain*, the dramatization of Somerset Maugham's *Miss Sadie Thompson*, the dramatic moment is the entrance of Sadie Thompson as her hard, blatant, vulgar self the morning after she has been "reformed and converted" by the missionary. In *Berkeley Square* there is the unforgettable last scene when the hero, returned to twentieth-century London after his miraculous visit to the past, is left alone with his memories of the girl he really loved, who has been dead a hundred and forty years. In *The Heiress* there is another unforgettable last scene when the heiress, who has agreed to elope with the fortune-hunting suitor who had jilted her two years before, bars the door against him and goes upstairs, leaving the stage empty as the curtain falls to the sound of furious and impatient pounding on the door.

One of the most impressive of serious-dramas is *The Green Pastures*. Based on Roark Bradford's stories *Ol' Man Adam an' His Chillun*, the play is a modern version of the medieval English Mystery plays, so called because each play or really playlet was presented by a mystery or trade guild; the complete cycle of plays told the story of the Bible from the creation to the ascension of Jesus into heaven. *The Green Pastures* tells these stories as understood by the simple Negroes of the deep South; the play has two threads of unity—the evolution in the character of God from the Lord of wrath and vengeance to one of love and suffering, and the vagaries of the Children of Israel, who offended their God so often, then begged forgiveness for their sins, only to sin again. No one who saw the play, the motion picture, or the television productions is likely to forget the heavenly fish fry, the entrance of the "Lawd" (as the angel Gabriel unctuously announces "Gangway for de Lawd God Jehovah!"), the scene in which God reveals himself to Noah, the tableau of the children of Israel on their way to the Promised Land, or the scene in the Babylonian night club where God announces he is through, he will have nothing more to do with his people. *The Green Pastures* remains one of the classics of American drama.

COMEDY-DRAMA

Not so serious as serious-drama, and yet not wholly a comedy, is the comedy-drama, which may be defined as *a play that combines the dramatic situation of serious-drama with the spirit of comedy, the emphasis being on the comedy.* One of the best examples of this type is Rostand's *Cyrano de Bergerac*, which, although usually classed as comedy or romantic comedy, has elements of seriousness out of keeping with pure comedy. Cyrano's love for Roxane, which he hides from her for fifteen years because of her love for Christian, her realization that it was Cyrano she had loved all the time, and his death in her arms, are dramatic and not comic subject matter. But in the main the spirit of comedy prevails in the play, expressed in Cyrano's characteristic actions and words, the references to his huge nose, especially his own brilliant speeches about it, and Christian's timidity and inability to tell his love.

They Knew What They Wanted, by Sidney Howard, is the story of a young girl who married an older man when she thought she was in love with another, a young man her own age. This Tristan and Isolde plot, which could be made into any type of play, was written as a fresh and interesting comedy-drama by not minimizing the seriousness of the situation, but at the same time treating it pleasantly and from a common-sense point of view. The wife soon realizes that she loves her husband, and is prepared to take her punishment for having wronged him; he, however, still loving his wife, is willing and eager to continue the marriage; he desires a home and a child, and will raise hers, even though he is not its father, if she will stay with him. Galsworthy's *Old English* is a comedy-drama written around the character of a rugged old Englishman of the last generation, and incidentally is a commentary on the changing order of the modern world—"Old English" definitely belongs to an older England, and would find men and conditions quite different were he to return today. *Disraeli*, by Louis N. Parker, although written about real persons and dealing with actual events, is a comedy-drama rather than a historical play, as the historical elements are subordinated to a main character partly true to life and partly a creation of the playwright, and to a story largely fiction. Other examples of comedy-drama are Saroyan's *The Time of Your Life*, De Hartog's *The Fourposter*, Wilder's *Our Town*, Thurber and Nugent's *The Male Animal*, Lindsay and Crouse's *State of the Union*, and McCullers' *Member of the Wedding*.

Serious-drama and comedy-drama are favorite media of the playwright of today, and the student of drama must recognize them as being almost of equal importance with the older forms of tragedy and comedy.

MELODRAMA

Melodrama (originally a play with music; perhaps the use of music in the motion pictures and television is the completion of a cycle) has always been regarded as the lowliest form of drama, fit only for the critic's scorn and laughter. As a matter of fact, melodrama is the carrying through of dramatic principles to their logical extremes. If drama is the art of play, or pretense, what more logical than that the hero achieve success no matter what the difficulties in his way, that the heroine be saved by and for him in spite of everything, and that the two be finally united against overwhelming odds? Melodrama goes to extremes as a sort of short cut to its goal, which is to reward the virtuous and punish the wicked; it eschews subtlety in favor of improbability, the more sensational the better. The hero is noble, brave, wise, and handsome, the heroine pure, sweet, courageous, and beautiful, the villain sinister, cruel, vindictive, and immoral—there is no half-way about any character type; and the result is that all heroes, heroines, and villains of melodrama are alike, and are types instead of individuals. Their adventures are of the hairbreadth kind that tend (and are intended) to send the chills down our spines—if the hero and the villain have a hand-to-hand battle, it is near the edge of a precipice; if the heroine is tied to the railroad track, the hero manages to get her free just a second before the train thunders past; if the heroine is being forced to marry the villain, the hero gets there not a minute too soon to claim her as his own. This is not life, but no one believes that it is. It is a show, and if its exaggerations offend the critical, its reversion to fundamentals in conflicts, characters, and situations appeals to an elemental side of us never far from the surface.

A melodrama is a serious-drama or a comedy-drama in which the characters are types rather than individuals, the story and situations exaggerated to the point of improbability or sensationalism, and the language and emotion over-emphasized and overdone. One of the best known melodramas is *After Dark, or Neither Wife, Maid, nor Widow,* by Dion Boucicault, revived some years ago by Christopher Morley. Audiences at the revival came prepared to laugh at the old-fashioned story, and enjoyed themselves doing so, but at the big scene, when the whole audience was in an uproar exhorting the faithful old friend to break through the wall in time to rescue the young man from the onrushing train, although many were shouting in a spirit of fun, there was also genuine concern for his safety. William Archer, for years England's ablest dramatic critic, whose translations of Ibsen had much to do with the renascence of English drama, wrote five plays, only one of which was successful—a melodrama. Although better written than the mine run of melodrama, with a distinctive villain for the protagonist (the role of the Rajah was identified with George Arliss, who created it and made it famous), *The Green Goddess* follows the standard formula for this type of play. Perhaps the most famous of all American melodramas is *Nellie, the Beautiful Cloak Model,* written with his tongue in his cheek, as a melodrama to end melodrama, by Owen Davis, who piled up the hairbreadth situations, crowding the play with traditional clichés. The villain misuses the heroine time and time again, only to ask her, in the last act, "Nellie, why do you fear me?" Expecting the audience to laugh at his play, the playwright was surprised to find it taking everything seriously. The play was a success, although not in the way intended, and made theatrical history. A recent example, *The Desperate Hours,* by Joseph Hayes, was a real thriller that kept audiences at the edge of their seats until the very end of the play. Melodrama has always been popular, and a good one will never lack an audience.

FARCE

Farce is to comedy what melodrama is to serious-drama. Melodrama exaggerates the dramatic to the point of sensationalism; farce exaggerates the comic to the point of absurdity. Farce, like melodrama, is not true to life; it is not concerned with realities, but with making audiences laugh. *A farce is a comedy in which the story, characters, and especially situations are so exaggerated that they pass from the realm of the probable to that of the improbable.* The writer of farce usually depends on rapidity of movement and ludicrousness of situation for his effects; absurd happenings seem more plausible in a fast-moving play filled with a series of events than in a slow-moving one built around a single situation.

Shakespeare's *Comedy of Errors* is a farce. The story of the long-separated twin brothers, with their twin servants, is too far-fetched to be convincing; but granted the premise, the two sets of identical twins and the relationship of master and man, the rest of the play follows logically. The result makes a more satisfactory play than one that starts with a plausible situation and gets more and more farcical as the play develops. Comedy and farce ordinarily do not mix, but in the hands of a master like Shakespeare the combination seems smooth and natural.

The Front Page, by Ben Hecht and Charles MacArthur, is a satiric farce on the newspaper business. The riotous events that occur in the newsmen's room in the Criminal Courts building while the reporters are waiting to write up the story of a hanging, especially the escape of the condemned man about to be executed and his capture by one of the reporters who locks him in a desk for safe-keeping until his paper can scoop the others, are too fantastic and unreal for comedy. But as rapid-fire farce the play is hilariously funny. *Boy Meets Girl,* by Samuel and Bella Spewack, is another satiric farce, this time on the motion pictures. The story is of two irresponsible script writers who adopt as their protege a little waitress who is going to have a baby. The studio publicizes her; "Happy," as she is going to name the baby, is assured of a leading part in a picture as soon as it is born; the baby later becomes a popular star and is paired with a famous "Western" actor; the waitress goes to high school to complete her education, and eventually marries the son of an English nobleman who has come to Hollywood to be an actor. Absurd as all this sounds, it is good farce material, and effectively satirizes certain aspects of the picture-making industry.

One of the best American farces is *Seven Keys to Baldpate,* as dramatized by George M. Cohan from the novel by Earl Derr Biggers. Besides this dramatization, there have been several motion-picture versions and a radio adaptation, but the play is superior to these, and in some ways to the novel itself. Although it has some comedy touches, the play is a true farce, with its mysterious visitors to the closed-up inn, each with what he believes to be the only key to the place, the package of money that changes hands many times, only to land in the fireplace to be burned up, the killing of the lady who afterward walks from room to room on the balcony, and the double surprise ending. *Arsenic and Old Lace,* by Joseph Kesselring, is a take-off on melodrama, in true farcical manner. Two delightful old ladies, sisters, take in lonely men as boarders, then poison them in order to insure their peace and quiet in the hereafter; their nephew, a gangster killer looking for a hideout, comes to their home; and there is a competition to see who can commit the most murders. It is all very delightful and ludicrously entertaining.

Farce and melodrama may not be so artistic as some other forms of drama, but they need not be slighted. If they tell their stories entertainingly, they are plays worthy of consideration.

HISTORY

A historical play is a serious attempt to re-create in dramatic form the life or part of the life of an actual person or period of history. The writer of historical plays takes all or most of his characters from the pages of history, although he often adds a few of his own invention to lighten or enhance his story. Distinction should be made between a play containing historical characters, like *Disraeli,* which is a comedy-drama with Disraeli as the protagonist, and a history containing fictional characters, like Shakespeare's *Henry IV,* in which Falstaff and his fellows are supplementary to the main plot (that Falstaff has become the chief figure of interest in the play and is always played by the leading actor does not alter the structure of the play, in which his story is the sub-plot). The aim of the play with historical characters is to tell a story made more dignified or authentic by the presence of famous persons; the aim of a historical play is to make history come to life.

The writer of a historical play, like the playwright who dramatizes a novel, always faces a double problem. He must produce a work acceptable to those familiar with the material, and he must also satisfy those who know little or nothing about it. Those who know the history involved in a play—say, about Queen Elizabeth, Abraham Lincoln, or Thomas à Becket—expect the playwright to be faithful to his sources and to include everything of importance, although at the same time he might omit many obvious references not necessary to their understanding of the story; those to whom the story is vague or unknown have a right to expect a play complete in itself, with not too much explanatory material that might become tiresome. The more familiar the historical figure is, of course, the more the playwright may take for granted, but he must steer a middle course, not taking too many liberties with the facts, nor yet being too repetitious in explaining what is already known.

Best of the historical plays in English are Shakespeare's, which have never been excelled for their vivid presentation of the English monarchs. In nine plays (excepting *King John,* the time of which is two hundred years earlier than the first of the series) we are given a bird's-eye view of English history from the reign of Richard II to that of Henry VIII, and so well are the kings brought to life that we remember them from the plays better than from history itself. Among modern historical plays should be mentioned: *Victoria Regina,* by Laurence Housman, a series of individual scenes, many of them personal and intimate glimpses, relating the life of Queen Victoria from her accession to her Diamond Jubilee; Maxwell Anderson's *Elizabeth the Queen* and *Mary of Scotland,* vigorous modern interpretations of their subject matter; *Murder in the Cathedral,* by T. S. Eliot, a poetical-mystical treatment of the Thomas à Becket story; and *Abe Lincoln in Illinois,* Robert E. Sherwood's Pulitzer Prize play, which deals with the life of Lincoln to the time he leaves for Washington to be inaugurated. Anderson's histories, like Shakespeare's, are written in the grand manner. *Victoria Regina* and *Abe Lincoln in Illinois* are "familiar" presentations of their characters, attempting to show them no less great, but more human. Writers of historical plays today often find in persons from the past spokesmen who can talk to us understandingly of present-day problems.

Chapter 8

LITERARY MOVEMENTS AND
REALITY IN DRAMA

EVERY AGE IN THE HISTORY OF DRAMA has contributed its share of
reality to the stage. When Aeschylus added the second actor to
Greek tragedy, and Sophocles the third, the stories told on the stage
were undoubtedly more realistic than they were when Thespis'
single actor talked with the Chorus. To the poetry-loving Elizabethans, Shakespeare's plays were very real, but many audiences
and readers of later ages found him out of fashion and unreal.
Samuel Pepys, as we learn from the diary, thought *A Midsummer-
Night's Dream* insipid and ridiculous, *Twelfth Night* one of the
weakest plays he ever saw, and *Romeo and Juliet* the worst play he
ever heard in his life. Examples nearer home may be found in the
accepted standards of acting of just a few years ago, when impas-
sioned declamation was considered the height of good acting, and
in the standard of the present, which prizes quietness and re-
straint.* Perhaps the most convincing example is in the motion
pictures, where the reality of yesterday is almost unbelievably
laughable today. Reality in the theater is constantly changing, and
much of what we consider real will no doubt seem unnatural to the
next generation.

The playwright, like the novelist, seeks to create an illusion of
reality in order that his work may seem convincing. The reader or
spectator must believe in the reality of the characters and the plot,
or he must be induced to suspend his disbelief for the time being,

* Compare, for instance, the phonograph records of E. H. Sothern in some
of his Shakespearean roles and those of Laurence Olivier or John Gielgud.
Sothern, who died in 1933, was considered one of the best Shakespearean
actors of his day.

or he must be put in the mood to be moved emotionally. As an artist, the playwright is concerned with the problem of relating his particular presentation to life itself, for whether the play is matter-of-fact or imaginative, a transcript of life or an interpretation, it is in some way a treatment of actuality. The illusion of reality may be created on the plane of everyday experience, by copying actuality in its outward detail, by presenting characters and events taken directly from life; on a plane of imaginative grandeur transcending actuality; or on a plane of deliberate distortion of the actual. The treatment of life on the everyday plane gives rise to realism and naturalism; on the plan transcending actuality it takes the form of romanticism or symbolism; and on the plane of distortion it becomes expressionism.

ROMANTICISM

Romanticism, revolting against both the sense of reality and the sense of society, moves on a plane of imaginative grandeur, and on that plane may compel a willing suspension of disbelief. Romanticism is not easy to define, but it may be said to represent the idealistic and imaginative side of man. Where classicism worships form, orderliness, and tradition, and realism stresses the practical, everyday details that add up to the whole of life, romanticism is indifferent to form and order, disregards tradition, and scorns the practical and everyday. The romantic spirit is expansive, exuberant, vibrant with life; it gives man high aspirations, and the vision and power to attain them or to try to attain them; it colors his existence with excitement and suspense. To the romanticist the unattainable and the unknowable are the most important things in the world.

Because the Elizabethan age was in the main romantic, and because Shakespeare was a great romanticist, romanticism became a reality on the English stage. Audiences saw two actors, both men, in exquisite love scenes, and instead of laughing at the absurdity of the situation, accepted the lovers as real; they saw boy actors who were supposed to be dainty fairies in a dream, and transported themselves to fairyland the better to enjoy the play; they saw kings and queens, from their own and other countries, in court and on the battlefield, come to life and make history before their eyes. But romanticism was not the only reality on the Elizabethan stage. Ben Jonson, who combined the qualities of classicism and realism, brought a fresh kind of illusion to English comedy, on the plane of everyday experience. The heroic play of the Restoration, with its love and honor theme, was romantic, although not on so high an imaginative plane as Shakespeare's plays; the comedy of manners was a form of realism. The Age of Reason went back to classicism, which became a reality in Addison's *Cato,* a typical eighteenth-century classical tragedy, and in Racine's tragedies. Shakespeare's plays, as presented on the Elizabethan stage, would have seemed utterly removed from reality in the eighteenth century; in fact, the polished and refined Age of Reason revised the plays to suit the new taste. The nineteenth century saw the romantic movement in full swing again, and once more romanticism was a reality in poetry and the drama. The twentieth century sees romanticism well established in the drama, although it is only one of several realities on the stage today.

The contributions of romanticism to the drama are many. From the Elizabethan panorama type of play came the use of many characters, in a variety of scenes. The unities of time and place were violated in favor of stories that gave full scope to the breadth of imagination. From Wordsworth and the romantic movement came the sense of wonder in everyday life, especially nature—

> And I have felt
> A presence that disturbs me with the joy
> Of elevated thoughts; a sense sublime
> Of something far more deeply interfused,
> Whose dwelling is the light of setting suns.

Plays of romantic love, of adventure, of man's deeds in the world of action, of the mystery of life—these and others like them owe their existence to romanticism.

The playwright of romanticism satisfies the desire of the audience to escape from the realities of life. Escapism explains why audiences will believe that Cyrano can fight one hundred men and defeat them and why Roxane can drive through enemy lines with provisions for her husband and his friends. The realist would scoff at such deeds and say they were impossible and beyond belief. *The Hairy Ape*, the realist would say, is more like life—what happens to Yank in the play is exactly what would happen to a man in real life under the given circumstances. The realist might allow Cyrano to fight several men and defeat them, but not a hundred, Roxane would never get through the Spanish lines, but if she did the carriage would have been searched first, and certainly no provisions would have been allowed to get to the besieged French. The romanticist would say these things are not to be taken too literally, but are symbolic of the chivalry and nobility of life. The romanticist, if he had written *The Hairy Ape*, after having Yank brood over Mildred's reaction to him, would have made a "new man" of Yank, he would have entered the world thus far closed to him, and eventually there would have been a happy marriage. Of course Rostand could never have written realistic drama any more than O'Neill could have written romantic drama. The two points of view are worlds apart.

TRADITION AND EXPERIMENT

In most ages there have been those who were satisfied with life and those who rebelled against it. Convention and tradition are always sufficient for some, a cause of unrest and challenge to others. Set fashions are ever subject to change by those who seek variety or improvement. Romanticism itself was a revolt, first against classicism, then against realism. The Age of Reason was a revolt, which in turn was revolted against; so also with the romantic movement. In fact, the pendulum seems endlessly swinging, as the liberal of one age becomes the conservative of the next, revolt merely sets up new conventions, and experiment creates new traditions.

Ibsen's early plays were written in the traditional manner, but *A Doll's House* was a revolt against the accepted dramatic standards of the time and marks the beginning of modern drama. *A Doll's House* is a milestone in the history of drama. For two and a half acts the play moves along in the manner of the "well-made"

play of the French school; then, when the original audiences probably thought it was coming to a close, it takes a sudden and unex-
pected twist, and modern drama, the drama of ideas, is born. In the
beginning of the play Nora is the doll-wife, Torvald the indulgent
but superior husband. He refers to her as his "squirrel," his "little
lark," his "little featherbrain." He laughs at her idea of borrowing
money on the strength of future income, but is solemnly serious
when he says, "Home life ceases to be free and beautiful as soon as
it is founded on borrowing and debt." That the inconsistency of this
attitude never occurs to him is a clear indication of his character.
He is fundamentally incapable of understanding Nora's reasons for
breaking the law; although his life was probably saved by
her action, he can not forgive her the disgrace she is bringing on
him. Ibsen's statement of the conflict between husband and wife
may be found in his "Notes for the Modern Tragedy": "There are
two kinds of spiritual law, two kinds of conscience, one in man and
another, altogether different, in woman. They do not understand
each other; but in practical life the woman is judged by man's law,
as though she were not a woman but a man."* The innovation lies
not in presenting the woman's point of view, which has often been
done, of course, in the drama, but in showing that the feminine
point of view in practical life has as much right to be heard as the
masculine, and is frequently likely to be more logical and clear-
sighted.

Nora's awakening is the turning point of the play. As Torvald
pours forth his vituperation against her, calling her a hypocrite,
liar, and criminal, a person who has betrayed his trust, who is not
fit to take care of her children, she listens calmly and quietly,
stunned by the revelation of his character, his total lack of understanding. When the message comes saying there will be no disgrace,
and Torvald utters his "I am saved! Nora, I am saved!" she asks,
with no change of expression, "And I?" The irony is lost on Torvald,
who magnanimously forgives her, and assures her that everything is
now all right. The play might have ended here, with the conventional happy ending. It would have been a typical well-made play,
no worse, and a good deal better, than most plays of its day. But it

* *From Ibsen's Workshop* (New York, John Wiley & Sons, 1911), p. 91.

would not have been a great play nor would it have been intellectually honest. For things have gone wrong between Nora and Torvald, and the solving of the material problem of the promissory note has in no way solved the spiritual problem confronting husband and wife. The scene that follows, the scene Ibsen had in mind from the beginning, is the most important; as the two sit at the table, facing each other, modern drama may be said to begin. The discussion of their marriage shows how Nora has changed from a doll-wife to a woman determined to find herself as a human being. A moment after she leaves the stage, "from below is heard the reverberation of a heavy door closing." The sound, as has been so often said, was heard around the world. Ibsen had not only liberated Nora, and through her millions of other women, but he had closed the door on the artificial, conventional drama of the time and shown the way to the new drama of ideas.

A new reality had come to the stage with *A Doll's House,* and the movement of realism in the drama was definitely under way. Later playwrights found that the reality of Ibsen did not go far enough for them, and they experimented with the form to find a more satisfactory method of expression by means of which they might tell their stories and say what they had to say. Present-day realism is a far cry from Ibsen's, which today seems quite conservative. Today's realistic playwrights stress the details of everyday life, building them up into a whole that strikes a responsive chord in audiences. William Inge's *Come Back, Little Sheba,* a most effective and appealing play, *The Dark at the Top of the Stairs,* and others of his plays illustrate the method well. If the critic objects that plays like these deal with trivia, even though the themes may be important ones, the playwrights would answer that life is made up of trivia and that their plays are a reflection of life.

REALISM AND NATURALISM

Both realism and naturalism are written on the theory that the only true illusion of reality is that which can be checked against actuality. Life is seen objectively, and presented on the plane of everyday experience. Realism is not systematic or methodical, but relies on the observation of the playwright, and may be colored by his likes and dislikes. Naturalism is more scientific in its method, and examines the facts impartially and impassively. Neither makes use of the Chorus or confidant, by means of which the playwright injects himself into the play, although realism often provides the *raisonneur* (a character created by nineteenth-century French playwrights to state the ideas of the play to the audience). The playwright of naturalism removes himself from the play as much as possible, presenting the facts without comment, like James Joyce, in whose novels the characters stand by themselves and speak for themselves, the author remaining completely out of the picture.

Realism and naturalism have been accused of ridiculing the idealistic and imaginative side of man, but emphasis on details does not necessarily mean lack of vision. The scientist who arranges his material and studies it does not allow emotion to affect his results, yet in the interpretation of his results he may be, and often is, the most idealistic and imaginative of men. The realist or naturalist tries to follow the scientist's use of the inductive method, and also his practice of dealing with fundamentals. If the realist or naturalist, although expert in the arrangement of details, lacks the scientist's imagination and vision, his presentation of life will seem pointless, and if the material is "basic" enough, even sordid. On the other hand, if he emphasizes vision and imagination, he will be trespassing in the province of the romantic, which, as a rebel against romanticism, he could never allow himself to do. Herein lies the weakness of the realism and naturalism of today—a too methodical arrangement of details will not make good drama, and an artistic arrangement defeats the purpose for which realism and naturalism exist. Early realists like Ibsen, Hauptmann, and Chekhov combined realism and artistry to write great plays; later realists and naturalists, relying more and more on the scientific method, are producing works interesting from the experimental point of view, but not great plays.

The objective method has had an effect on dramatic technique. The stress on details has caused action and plot to seem of minor importance. The emphasis is on character, which is presented not dynamically, developing through a turning point to a climax, but in one phase of development; it is not the story of the character so much as his state of mind at a particular time that interests the play-wright. The character is shown, usually with others who are of equal importance in the play, in relation to his background. Instead of one or two protagonists, interest is divided among several, even many, characters; their common enemy is poverty, heredity, society, or the world. In other words, the main conflict is that of the individual against outside forces. The dialogue in which this conflict is related is supposedly as much like the language of real life as possible, but actually the playwright uses selection here as he does everywhere else in drama. Realism and naturalism have brought lifelike dialogue to the stage, but not life itself—only the illusion of reality. A realistic or naturalistic play is first and foremost a play.

The contribution of Ibsen to the illusion of reality in the drama has already been mentioned. Hauptmann combined the objective method with tense dramatic situations; his plays are among the most powerful of the realistic school. Chekhov's contribution was to combine technical skill with the "slice of life" play, in which very little happens, the characters walking about and talking quietly of their affairs. Yet for all their seeming lack of structure, the plays of Chekhov contain (or perhaps a better word would be conceal) the highest artistry. The influence of these three playwrights has been considerable, in the drama of realism and in drama generally.

Maxim Gorki went a step further. He maintained that a play-wright is like a host at a party, who records the words and actions of his guests without in any way injecting his own ideas or feelings; he must "cold-bloodedly describe the manner in which they all behave." Gorki later said that he had never and could never do this, and that he knew of no European play written according to this theory. We know that a tape recorder hidden in a roomful of characters who talked unrestrainedly for two hours would not record a play, because the hand of the artist is absent. *The Lower Depths* is in the main grimly realistic, but in the character of Luka, the pilgrim who comes mysteriously into the lives of the characters, has some influence on them, and then as mysteriously disappears, we note the element of romanticism, already mentioned as often being present in realistic plays.

Two excellent examples of modern realism are Sidney Kingsley's *Dead End* and Elmer Rice's *Street Scene*. The audience at each play found itself looking at a real street scene—there was no question about the reality of the setting or the acting. The setting for *Dead End* is a New York street ending at the East River; the "Dead End Kids," who played in the original production later became famous as portrayers of street urchins. The play tells about the lives of those who live in the tenement district on the East Side, especially the gang of tough boys who make the street their headquarters, and also about "Babyface" Martin, who once lived on the street but left it to become a gangster. Good as the play is, it reveals the weakness as well as the strength of realism. The conflicts between the gang of boys and the wealthy boy who lives in the fashionable apartment house with its terrace bordering on the street, and those between the gang and the law, belong properly to realism, as does the conflict between the gangster and his former sweetheart, now a streetwalker. But the conflict between the gangster and the G-men who are looking for him and finally kill him is melodramatic, and the love of Gimpty, the idealist with the twisted leg, who is in a way the playwright's spokesman, and Kay is romantic. Apparently the playwright was not content to build a play with realistic elements alone. *Street Scene* is more consistently realistic, although it too makes use of romanticism, with the love story of the idealistic young law student and the girl whose father kills her mother because she is unfaithful. That both these plays should add a romantic touch is an indication of the inadequacy of the objective method, at least as far as these two playwrights are concerned.

Naturalism is realism followed to its logical extreme, and with an added philosophy of materialism. The playwright of naturalism is not only coldly scientific in his treatment of actuality, but his outlook is entirely materialistic. In his search for basic material he goes to the elemental in life. Using the objective method systematically, he prides himself on calling a spade a spade; the result is not a pretty picture for the squeamish, who find naturalism objectionable, even obscene. Human nature is at its lowest in *King Lear*; yet a naturalistic play like *Tobacco Road* makes life seem baser and much less dignified. The reason lies partly, of course, in the language used by naturalism, and partly in the case-history-attitude of the playwright, who attempts to show evil, not as the romanticist does, in conflict with good, which eventually triumphs, but as an established force, which is to be reckoned with, examined, and if possible, explained.

Tobacco Road, dramatized by Jack Kirkland from the novel by Erskine Caldwell, like many realistic and naturalistic plays, is a study of family life; the family, rather than an individual, is the protagonist. The main conflict deals with the Lesters, a lazy, degenerate, "white trash" family in the back country of Georgia, and their struggle to keep themselves alive. There is little action. Pearl, one of the Lester children, a mere child, has run away from her husband, who comes to take her back; the Lesters steal his turnips and gorge themselves on the first real food they have had in days. Sister Bessie, a buxom, middle-aged, man-loving itinerant preacher, marries herself (performing her own ceremony) to Duke Lester, a boy of sixteen, who is more attracted to the new car she buys him than to her person. The former owner of the land and the representative of the bank which now owns it come to dispossess Jeeter and his family unless they can pay rent. Pearl's husband offers Jeeter a weekly sum if Pearl will return to him; Ada, Pearl's mother, takes her part, and tells Jeeter that Pearl is not his daughter. At the end of the play Ada has been run over and killed by Duke in the new car, Pearl has run away to the city, another daughter has been sent by Jeeter to the cabin of the deserted husband to console him, and Jeeter himself, alone on his land, hopes he will be allowed to remain there. With the exception of the two city men, brought in for the sake of contrast, each character is a full-blooded person about whom a story might have been centered, even the shadowy Grandma, who scarcely says a word, but wanders furtively in and out searching for food and fuel and avoiding the abuse of the others. *Tobacco Road* is an honest attempt to present a section of American life.

SYMBOLISM AND EXPRESSIONISM

Symbolism and expressionism represent reactions against realism and naturalism. Symbolism is telling two stories at the same time, an outer or concrete one, and a parallel inner or abstract one. The symbolist tries to capture the plane on which the older romantic drama moved, and he also would appeal to the interest in serious problems by super-imposing the method of the double story. Not satisfied with the conventional method of expressing the theme of his play, he objectifies it; in other words, instead of the theme being an idea that the plot illustrates, as is usual in most plays, the theme is expressed as another, the inner, plot. The double meaning is the source of symbolism's particular effect, although it has its dangers—the reality of the outer plot is often distorted in order to fit the needs of the inner plot; and the inner plot, if it becomes too objective, may turn the play into propaganda or preachment.

Symbolism as a method of expression should not be confused with the use of symbols as a dramatic device, although one is the natural development from the other. The storm scenes in *King Lear* are symbolic, as is the orphanage in *Ghosts*, but the plays themselves are not symbolic, because the inner meaning is not objectified to make a story parallel to the outer plot. Ibsen's later plays, however, are symbolic, the inner and outer stories running parallel through the play.

Symbolism is not new in the drama. The old morality plays, like *Everyman* or *The Castle of Perseverance*, with their personified characters—Everyman, Death, Good Deeds, Knowledge, Experience, Ignorance, Pride, Patience, Truth, and so on—are among the best examples of the symbolic play, and the easiest to understand. Other plays in which the symbolism is easy to follow are Barrie's *Peter Pan*, Rostand's *Chantecler*, Maeterlinck's *The Blue Bird*, Hauptmann's *The Assumption of Hannele* (in these plays the device of fantasy is used as a means of objectifying the theme), Kennedy's *The Servant in the House*, and Jerome's *The Passing of the Third Floor Back*. In the two last-named plays the inner story so dominates the outer that the characters seem almost like puppets; the simplification and emphasis of the symbolism has caused a distortion of reality in the outer plot (in *The Passing of the Third Floor Back*, the ease with which the Stranger influences the persons in the boarding house and their complete change from bad to good are not very real), which we are willing to accept because of the sincerity and earnestness of the playwright in presenting his theme. Symbolism is usually more concerned with the message it has to offer than with the story it has to tell.

Plays in which symbolism is not so easy to follow, but is open to more than one interpretation, are Ibsen's *Rosmersholm* and *The Master Builder*, Maeterlinck's *The Intruder* and *The Blind*, and Hauptmann's *The Sunken Bell*. In these plays the degree of distortion in the outer plot seems to depend upon the interpretation of the theme. To some the inner story of *Rosmersholm* or of *The Master Builder* admits of simple interpretation, so that the outer story may be enjoyed almost solely for its own sake. To others the symbolism is so involved that nearly every speech and action of the characters is thought to contain an inner significance. In *The Intruder, The Blind,* and *The Sunken Bell,* the interpretation is complicated by the mysticism of the theme; reality has taken on a dreamlike quality in keeping with the inner story.

The Blue Bird may be taken as representative of the symbolic play. The theme is the search for happiness, objectified in the Blue Bird, sought by the two children Tyltyl and Mytyl. Using the device of fantasy, the playwright shows these children of a poor woodcutter being visited by the Fairy Berylune, who commands them to bring her the Blue Bird. To aid them in the search, she gives them a magic diamond, by means of which they may look into the past and the future, and also into the inside of things. As companions on their journey they have Light, Bread, Sugar, Fire, Water, Milk, the Dog, and the Cat, all of whom come to life as real persons when the diamond, which sees things as they are, calls forth their souls. The children, with these companions, visit the Land of Memory, the Palace of Night, the Forest, the Palace of Happiness, the Graveyard, and the Kingdom of the Future. The Blue Bird is not to be found, although the children meet their grandparents, long dead, who are aroused from their sleep every time someone in the land of the living thinks of them, they are attacked by the trees, who, once the diamond has made them articulate, would have revenge on their enemy Man; in the Graveyard they discover, with the aid of the diamond, that there are no dead; in the Kingdom of the Future everything is blue, including hundreds of birds, some of which they capture, only to see them change color later. Light is their chief friend and guide; Bread and Sugar give them food when they are hungry; and the faithful Dog and the treacherous Cat reveal their true selves (to the audience—the children, true to human nature, do not appreciate faithfulness, and are taken in by hypocrisy masking treachery). At the end of their journey, which turns out to be a dream, they are home again, and they find the Blue Bird in Tyltyl's turtle dove, which had been in its cage all the time.

As in all symbolic plays, the inner story is the important one. The playwright would tell us that happiness is elusive, and difficult of attainment. We may think we have secured it, but we are always disillusioned. We ourselves are Tyltyl, who says, "The one of the Land of Memory turned quite black, the one of the Future turned quite pink, the Night's are dead, and I could not catch the one in the Forest. Is it my fault if they change color, or die, or escape?" Light answers, "We have done what we could. It seems likely that the Blue Bird does not exist or that he changes color when he is caged." But the Blue Bird does exist, and when the neighbor, who looks a great deal like the Fairy Berylune, comes to ask Tyltyl for his turtle dove that her little sick daughter has been longing to possess, he gladly gives it up. A moment later the neighbor returns with her little girl, whom the gift has made well. Tyltyl explains to the child, who bears a strong resemblance to Light, "I have seen bluer ones. But those which are quite blue, you know, do what you will, you can't catch them." As they are admiring the bird, it escapes and flies away; Tyltyl comforts the little girl—"Never mind. Don't cry. I'll catch him again." Then he turns to the audience and says, "If any of you should find him, would you be so kind as to give him back to us? We need him for our happiness later on." So the search is never-ending. Happiness is in the past, in the future, wherever we may be; but it must be sought and striven for, and it usually is fleeting. It is to be found right at home, as well as in far-off places, but only through experience do we learn this simple truth. It is the search for happiness, more than its attainment, that the play emphasizes.

The Blue Bird objectifies its theme without at the same time sacrificing the outer story, which is entertainingly told and contains many of the familiar devices of drama. The kindly friend, who always appears in time to help in a crisis, the hypocritical friend secretly conspiring, the plot thwarted at the last moment by another faithful friend, and the element of surprise in addition to suspense (in the graveyard scene), make an effective play. The success of *The Blue Bird* is due largely to the symbolism, with its universal appeal, but partly to the technical skill of the playwright.

A more recent effective use of symbolism is to be found in the plays of Tennesee Williams. The title of *The Glass Menagerie* indicates the importance of the symbolism. Laura is a fragile person, living a sheltered life in a world apart, just like her little glass animals. When one of the figures is broken, it is more than an accident—it is illusion coming into contact with reality. And it is not only Laura who lives in a world of illusion—her mother Amanda, and her brother Tom, who narrates the story, also live in a world of their own making. In *A Streetcar Named Desire* the shaded lamp and darkened room which Blanche insists on are symbolic of her shrinking from the facts of her life; when Mitch wishes to see her as she really is, he tears off the lampshade and turns the light up. In *Summer and Smoke* the symbolic touch is in the lighting up of the statue of the Angel several times in the play. If Laura, Blanche, and Alma (of *Summer and Smoke*) are really the same person, as some maintain, they are symbolic not only of decaying southern aristocracy but of a cultural element in the world that is in danger of becoming lost.

Expressionism is a modern attempt to reduce dramatic action and narrative progression to a discontinuous sequence of ideationally controlled episodes. An extreme form of symbolism, it tries to move for the most part on a new plane, one that is neither actuality nor the plane of the older romantic drama. The expressionist attempts to create the illusion of reality on a plane of deliberate distortion of actuality, presenting the inner story of the symbolism with little or no dependence on the outer, which loses semblance to real life and is the starting place for the playwright's imagination. Expressionistic plays have two things in common. First, they deal with the disordered thinking, the uncertain values, and the striving to adjust oneself in a bewildering world that seem a definite part of the modern age. Playwrights of expressionism, concerned with setting forth the picture of a world utterly different from that of the past, have evolved a medium of presentation equally new. The outer story is not a continuous one, with each scene advancing the plot a step, but rather a series of scenes loosely joined, each of which is a part of the picture as a whole. In the second place, expressionistic plays depend a good deal on the visual and aural, which require actual performance to be really effective. Expressionism does not produce great literature, but it does produce striking scenic effects that are long remembered as truly interpretative of the emotion or idea they are intended to portray.

In O'Neill's *The Hairy Ape* the later scenes grow increasingly imaginative and grotesque, as the playwright gives us not reality, but the world as seen through the disordered mind of the sailor. The scene on Fifth Avenue, with the mechanical, puppetlike characters, represents not an actual happening, but an idea. *Processional*, by John Howard Lawson, is like a series of vaudeville scenes, most of them about to break up into a song-and-dance act or a spectacular tableau. Such scenes are a new departure in drama; the playwright is attempting to reproduce, in his own medium, the "stream of consciousness" effect of James Joyce and his school. Reality is sacrificed for the sake of idea or emotion.

The best American expressionistic play is Elmer Rice's *The Adding Machine*, which protrays man caught in the toils of the machine age like an animal trapped in a cage. We first see Mr. Zero (the protagonist) in his bedroom, where his wife, in a long monologue, berates him for his twenty-five years in the same position in the same office, Mr. Zero, all the while, uttering not a word. The next scene is in the office, showing Mr. Zero and his fellow clerk, Miss Devore, at work. In this scene the only setting is a circular platform, in the center of the stage; on one side of a desk, on a high book-keeper's stool, sits Mr. Zero, and opposite him, on another stool, sits Miss Devore. A light shines on the platform and the two clerks; the rest of the stage is dark. As they sit facing each other, doing their work mechanically, they also speak their thoughts, in the manner used later in O'Neill's *Strange Interlude*. Mr. Zero, sex-starved all his life, has a sneaking fondness for Miss Devore, we learn, although outwardly he scarcely seems to notice her existence. She, also sex-starved, is in love with him, but similarly gives no sign. A whistle blows, marking the end of the working day. Miss Devore leaves. The Boss enters to talk with Mr. Zero, not to offer him a raise in salary, as he had hoped, but to tell him that the firm is installing machines to do his work, and that therefore he will no longer be needed. Mr. Zero's anger slowly rises at the injustice of being discharged after twenty-five years, and the platform begins slowly to revolve, with the accompaniment of soft music. As Mr. Zero's anger mounts, the platform moves more and more rapidly, and the voices of the two men are drowned in the music, which gets louder and louder. "To it is added every off-stage effect of the theater: the wind, the waves, the galloping horses, the locomotive whistle, the sleigh bells, the automobile siren, the glass-crash," ending in a terrific peal of thunder. Then a flash of red, "and then everything is plunged into blackness." Without a doubt this is one of the most effective scenes in expressionistic drama; it serves its purpose admirably, for in no other way could the playwright so succinctly present Mr. Zero's state of mind as he rebels for the first time in his life.

The third scene is in the Zeros' living room, where some friends (Messrs. One, Two, Three, Four, Five, and Six, "and their respective wives") have come to spend the evening. The dialogue is often deliberately mechanical, especially when several of the characters speak in unison. At the end of the scene the police arrest Mr. Zero for the murder of the Boss. The fourth scene shows the trial, and is another excellent example of expressionism. The setting is three bare white walls; at one side is a jury-box, in which are seated Messrs One, Two, Three, Four, Five, Six, "and their respective wives." The jury listens stolidly, staring before them, as Mr. Zero tells his story. The whole scene consists of one long speech by Mr. Zero, which is interrupted when the jurors suddenly relax, look at each other, whisper among themselves, then rise and shout in unison "GUILTY!" A comparison with a realistic trial scene, such as in the same playwright's *On Trial*, Galsworthy's *Justice*, Edward Wooll's *Libel!*, or the Perry Mason courtroom scenes, will show that expressionism, although it distorts the facts, yet presents its own kind of reality.

The remaining three scenes show Mr. Zero's life after death. He meets Miss Devore, who has killed herself for love of him, but he is too much the weakling to grasp happiness, even when it is held out to him. In the last scene he is in an office again, this time working on a huge machine, happy to be its attendant; but his new boss tells him that he must go back to earth and start life all over. He learns that he has been in heaven a number of times. The first time, thousands of years ago, he had been a monkey. "You weren't so bad as a monkey." Then he had hauled stones for one of the pyramids; he had been a Roman galley slave; a thousand years after that he had been a serf—"You wore an iron collar then —white ones hadn't been invented yet." Always he went a step down. His next job on earth will be to operate a "superb, super-hyper-adding machine."

DISILLUSIONMENT

A recent school of playwrights has been writing what may be called the drama of disillusionment. These playwrights are angry and disappointed young men, some of them of the "Beat" generation, who see the world in a sad state because of the mismanagement and mistakes of the older generation. Among the plays of disillusionment and frustration are John Osborne's *Look Back in Anger*, Samuel Beckett's *Waiting for Godot*, and Eugene Ionesco's *The Chairs*. These plays are characteristic of an age such as ours with its uncertainties and complexities, its cold war, its outer space experiments, but the plays of this school do not really seem part of the main stream of drama. The frustration is not the gentle, universal frustration of Chekhov, or the fundamental, philosophical frustration of O'Neill; the anger does not have the sparkle or the bite of Shaw. The angry young men somehow give the impression that they are angry only temporarily, that their future, more mature work will perhaps be more tolerant of the weaknesses of mankind.

The various dramatic movements of the last hundred years or so, realism, naturalism, symbolism, expressionism, and others that might have been mentioned, such as the existentialism of Jean-Paul Sartre and the "epic theater" of Berthold Brecht, are part of what is known as the experimental theater, which is interested in breaking away from tradition. New York has its off-Broadway theater, where the unusual and different drama may be seen. The experimental drama is noteworthy for two reasons. It proves that the drama is still very much alive, that it is not set in its ways, that it will continue to develop and evolve. But a careful study of the experimental theater also reveals that it is not so experimental as it may seem, that the basic principles of the drama have not changed very much since the Greeks, that the playwright will always deal with man's conflict with other men, with himself, or with a superior force. The purpose of drama will always be to entertain, the aim will be to tell a story entertainingly. The art of the playwright will always combine with the art of the actor to please the audience.

Chapter 9

❧

HOW TO JUDGE A PLAY

A COMMON MISTAKE of the uncritical is to expect too much from a work of only modest pretensions, or to take for granted that a work planned on an ambitious scale must be good. An epic poem is undeniably greater than a sonnet, but the same standards will not serve for both. If a composer writes a symphony, or a playwright attempts a play in the Shakespearean manner, he is inviting the most severe criticism—his work must be compared with the best in the field. A simple song, however, is not to be compared with a symphony, and a modest little comedy should be compared, not with the plays of Aristophanes, Jonson, or Molière, but with other modest little comedies. The artist must be judged on what he has tried to do, and the way he has done it. A little work perfectly executed is more artistic than a big work badly executed. The value to the world of any work is usually decided, in the long run, by the world itself, and it is in the province of the critic to anticipate the final verdict.

Criticism is itself an art, and one who wishes to study it seriously must undergo a long period of training. To understand what the artist is trying to do, the trained critic must familiarize himself with the artist and the period of which he is a part; to judge how well the work has been done, the trained critic must possess a thorough knowledge of technique; and to decide if the work was worth doing, he must have a true sense of values. But one need not be a trained critic in order to criticize systematically. With a little practice anyone may become a critic, if he has good taste, the power of discrimination, and a wholesome supply of common sense.

A play may be judged either as a work of art in itself, or as a finished theatrical production played before an audience. Obviously there are different criteria for each. To begin with, how are we to judge a play as a literary work, irrespective of its performance on the stage?

THE PRINTED PLAY

To judge a play as a literary work we should ask the following question about it:

(1) *Purpose and Aim.* The first question to ask about a play is, What is the playwright's intention? We know that in general the purpose of a play is to entertain, and the aim is to tell a story, but we also know that behind the entertainment and the story is usually an idea, often the real reason for the play's being. Why has the playwright written the play? Has he some ideas to expound, a philosophy of life to present? Is his intention to give a picture of the life of the time? Is he merely giving way to a desire for self-expression? Is the play mainly a vehicle for an actor or a director? Is the playwright's chief interest in technique? Is his purpose only to entertain or amuse? The intention may be the answer to one of these questions, or the combined answers to several.

The next question is, Has the playwright fulfilled his intention? Has he succeeded in what he started out to do? Does the play realize the potentialities of its type, that is, the fundamental effects of tragedy, comedy, serious-drama, and so on? If the play sets out to be a tragedy, is it a true tragedy, or is it a serious-drama with an unhappy ending? If it sets out to be a comedy, is the comic effect kept to the fore, or is it made subordinate to some other element that would be more fitting in another type of play? If a playwright intends to write a melodrama, he should not be criticized because his play is not a serious-drama; but if he writes serious-drama that turns into melodrama, he is confusing the two types. There is no reason why several types of drama may not be combined, and they frequently are, sometimes successfully. The critic must be able to separate the various elements in a combination, and he must decide whether the combination is inad-

vertent or intentional. The major playwrights may usually be
depended upon to fulfill their intention scrupulously.

(2) *Theme*. The next questions to ask about a play, and sometimes they overlap the questions about intention, are, What is the
theme and what is its value? The great plays have significant
themes, of universal and lasting interest—filial ingratitude, as in
King Lear; a great self-effacing love, as in *Cyrano*; woman's right
to live as an individual, as in *A Doll's House;* or the search for
happiness, as in *The Blue Bird*. A good theme does not necessarily
make a good play, as there are other elements to be considered,
but a good play based on a good theme is better than a good play
based on a poor theme. A play without a theme is not worth
serious criticism.

(3) *Plot*. Every play should tell a story, so the next questions
to ask are, Is the plot a good one. Is it convincing? Is it true to
life, or at least true to the kind of life it attempts to portray? and
finally, Is it a good illustration of the theme? To be good, a plot
must be unhackneyed, not using trite situations that have been
used a thousand times, it must ring true, and it must be a just
and logical presentation of the theme. The story of King Lear
fulfills the requirements of a good plot, although the original
division of the kingdom is a little implausible, and the two daughters are so wicked that it is a little difficult to believe in them;
but the repetition of the main plot in the story of Gloucester and
his sons shows us that filial ingratitude is a universal situation.
The plots of *Cyrano* and *A Doll's House* fit their themes well, even
if the fifteen years' silence of Cyrano and the forging of the signa-
ture by Nora incline slightly toward the melodramatic. The search
for happiness has been the theme of many plays; *The Blue Bird*
presents it in a fantasy. Here the question to ask is not, Is the
story true to life? for it is not meant to be. But, accepting the
fantasy, we must ask, Is the story consistent, faithful to the main
idea? Fantasies like *The Blue Bird*, *Chantecler*, *Peter Pan*, and
others, are convincing on their own levels; they are true to life in
that make-believe world which the playwright has created. Plots
that are not good illustrations of their themes are, as we have

already seen, *The Second Mrs. Tanqueray* and *Abie's Irish Rose*.*
The best plots are those that are interesting in themselves, and
also realize fully the significance of the theme.

(4) *Characters.* The great playwrights create characters that
live, that do not merely utter speeches that their author puts into
their mouths, but seem to have a life of the their own, saying
memorable things that linger in the mind of the reader. The
questions to ask about characters are, Are they real human beings?
Are they individuals, not types? and Are their speech and actions
logical, convincing, and worth remembering? Plays with good
themes and plots often have lifeless or colorless characters, or
type characters that have been used repeatedly; on the other
hand, if the theme and plot of a play are weak, good characters
can do much to redeem it.

(5) *Technique.* The fifth and last matter to consider is technique, under which we may consider the way the play is put
together, as described in Chapter 4, and the dialogue. Does the
story move smoothly and easily? Is it interesting throughout, or
does it drag through dull moments? Is the first act good? The
rising action? The turning point? The climax? Are the dramatic
situations well written and handled? Is the ending satisfying, or
is it a let-down from the rest of the play? Is the dialogue pertinent
and convincing? Is it stilted, wooden, lifeless, unpleasing, or is
it easy and natural, alive, with the neat turn of phrase that indicates
a master of style? Is it a fitting medium for the story it has to tell?

One who can answer the foregoing questions intelligently when
he reads a play is already a critic. Until he becomes familiar with
them, he should read a play with the questions before him, but
he will soon find that reading critically comes easily. As his knowledge and experience increase, additional questions will come to
mind. How does the play compare with the playwright's other
works? What is its importance in the literature and thought of the
day? If the play is by a new and unknown playwright, how does
it compare with other plays of the past or present? What are the
distinguishing characteristics of the new playwright, and how is

* See Chapter 3.

he to be rated? What is the opinion of other critics on the play in
question, and what is the explanation of any differences of opinion?

THE ACTED PLAY

To judge a play as a finished theatrical production, played before
an audience, we must supplement the questions asked about the
play itself with questions relating to three additional elements.
We must first learn to distinguish between the play as written and
the play as we see it in the theater. If we read a play first and
then see it acted, or if we are familiar with plays like Shakespeare's
or Ibsen's when we go to see them, the distinction is not so difficult
to make. But usually we go to the theater knowing little or nothing
about the play beforehand, and it is easy to confuse excellence
in acting with excellence in authorship, or to miss the good
qualities of a play because of an inferior production. As has already
been stated,* the four contributions in the making of a theatrical
performance are those of the playwright, the actor, the producer,
and the audience. Theoretically the playwright's share is finished
when he delivers his play to the producer, whose business it is to
bring the play to life on the stage. What are the questions to ask
about the acting, the production, and the audience?

Next to the playwright, the actor is most important when the
play is presented. Is he convincing in his role? Does he make the
character live, so that we believe in him? Is his voice resonant, his
enunciation clear? Does he have a personality, a stage presence?
Great actors of the past and present have shown that the answers
may be yes to all these questions. Lesser actors have weaknesses
somewhere. And of course actors are better in some roles than in
others. Finally we must ask, What has the play done for the actor,
and what has the actor done for the play?

The producer is responsible for the direction and the staging of
the play. Are the actors well cast? Are all the roles carefully and
artistically presented? Do the actors play together well, striving
for a unified effect for the sake of the play as a whole, or do certain
of them try to "hog" their parts? Does the scenery give the fullest

* P. 18.

expression to the play's meaning and mood, is it too elaborate, or is it inadequate? A good producer leaves a distinguishing mark on a play, which in the hands of a poor producer might be a colorless failure.

Last is the contribution of the audience, whose responsiveness must be taken into account in any evaluation of an acted play. Has the audience paid the play the perfect compliment of rapt attention and complete absorption? Or has its attention wandered, is it glad of the intermissions, is it in haste to leave at the end of the play? The size and type of audience is also important. Although an inferior play may draw crowds and a great play draw empty houses, and thus attendance be far from an accurate measuring stick, still a play that everyone comes to see deserves some credit, and a play that nobody cares to see must have something wrong with it. At the same time, a small appreciative audience is worth more in the estimation than a large indifferent one. Our common sense must help us here.

The three elements of acting, staging, and audience must be considered along with the play to arrive at an evaluation of the finished production. A fine production of a fine play is always a memorable experience for all concerned. A poor production may spoil a good play; a good production may improve a poor play.

This brings us to another question: Which is preferable, and offers more enjoyment, a great play poorly acted or a mediocre play greatly acted? The great plays are always worth seeing, and some think that it is better to see them acted poorly than not at all. On the other hand, great acting is rare indeed and is a delight to watch, even in a poor play. Although it may sound strange, the preference from the critical standpoint should be for great acting. Inadequate acting of a great play causes a feeling of insufficiency, of disappointment. Great acting of an inferior play (not of a poor play, however, where the great acting would only be wasted) may cause regret that the play is no better, but there will be no disappointment with that particular performance. The play is the constant, the production the variable. A first-rate actor in almost anything is more enjoyable than a second- or third-rate production of *Hamlet, Antigone,* or *Ghosts.*

As we become proficient in judging a play, we will think less and less of each element separately, and more and more of the play or production as a whole. We will discover that there is something about a play that defies analysis—that the whole is greater than the sum of its parts. What that indefinable something is, what makes one play distinguishable from all others, is part of the final appraisal; and intelligent appraisal of a play is an important part of the enjoyment of drama.

BIBLIOGRAPHY

THIS LIST CONTAINS SUGGESTIONS for those who wish to read further in the study of drama. Among the large number of works on the subject, each of the following will be found useful and interesting. Many of the modern studies of the drama, and especially some of the collections of plays, have excellent bibliographies of their own, which should be consulted if fuller lists are desired.

Aristotle's *Poetics* is the starting place of dramatic criticism and should be read in a good translation, preferably that of S. H. Butcher or Lane Cooper. Barrett Clark's *European Theories of the Drama* (revised edition) contains most of the *Poetics*, and also selections from the criticism of Horace, Sidney, Jonson, Lessing, Brunitière, Coleridge, and others, along with a few American critical writings, including those of O'Neill, Anderson, and Rice. George Saintsbury's *History of English Criticism* gives a full account of English critics to about 1900; English dramatic criticism may be studied in A. C. Ward's *Specimens of English Dramatic Criticism, XVII–XX Centuries.* There are popular reprints of such writers as Sidney, Jonson, Dryden, Coleridge, Hazlitt, Lamb, and Meredith, whose *Essay on Comedy* is one of the most important on the subject. More recent works on criticism in general are *Critical Approaches to Literature,* by David Daiches, and *Literary Criticism: A Short History,* by William K. Wimsatt, Jr., and Cleanth Brooks, which is likely to remain the standard history of criticism for some time to come.

The best modern studies of the art of the drama are *Playmaking,* by William Archer; *Dramatic Technique,* by G. P. Baker; *The Theory of Drama,* by Allardyce Nicoll; *Drama,* by Ashley Dukes; *Theory and Technique of Playwriting,* by J. H. Lawson; *Write That Play* and *A Theater in Your Head,* by Kenneth Rowe; *The Playwright as Thinker,* by Eric Bentley; *The Idea of a Theatre,* by Francis Fergusson; *Anatomy of Criticism,* by Northrup Frye; *The Spirit of Tragedy,* by Herbert Muller; and *Elements of Drama,* by J. L. Styan. Good general surveys of the history of drama are *The Development of Dramatic Art,* by D. G. Stuart; *A Short History of the Drama,* by M. F. Bellinger; *The Development of the Theater, British Drama,* and *World Drama,* by Allardyce Nicoll; *British Drama,* by Alan Downer; *Tragedy* and *English Comedy,* by A. H. Thorndyke; *Masters of English Comedy*, by H. T. E. Perry; *Masters of the Drama* (third edition), by John Gassner; and *The Theater: Three Thousand Years of Drama, Acting, and Stagecraft*, by Sheldon Cheney. An excellent general reference is the *Oxford Companion to the Theatre*, edited by Phyllis Hartnoll.

More detailed studies of periods are *The Attic Theatre* and *The Tragic Drama of the Greeks*, by A. E. Haigh; *Greek Tragedy*, by H. D. F. Kitto; *The Drama of the Medieval Church*, by Karl Young; *The Medieval Stage* and *The Elizabethan Stage*, by E. K. Chambers; *Shakespeare's Predecessors in the English Drama*, by J. A. Symonds; *Elizabethan Drama*, by F. E. Schelling; *Introduction to Tudor Drama* and *Introduction to Stuart Drama*, by F. S. Boas (both very good); *Elizabethan and Jacobean Playwrights*, by H. B. Wells; *A Short View of Elizabethan Drama*, by T. M. Parrott and R. H. Ball; *A Life of William Shakespeare*, by J. Q. Adams; *The Globe Playhouse*, by J. C. Adams; *Shakespearean Tragedy*, by A. C. Bradley (one of the best books ever written on Shakespeare); *Shakespeare* by John Masefield (an excellent brief work); *Prefaces to Shakespeare*, by Harley Granville-Barker (highly recommended); *Shakespeare*, by Mark van Doren; *The Art and Life of William Shakespeare*, by Hazelton Spencer; *Shakespeare of London*, by Marchette Chute (interesting romantic biography); *Shakespeare's Historical Plays* and *The Elizabethan World Picture*, by E. M. W. Tillyard (the latter a must for all lovers of the Elizabethan period); *As They Liked It*, by Alfred Harbarge; *The Irresistible Theatre*, by W. Bridges-Adams; *The Jacobean Drama*, by Una Ellis-Fermor; *History of Restoration Drama*, by Allardyce Nicoll; *Restoration Tragedy* and *Restoration Comedy*, by Bonamy Dobrée (collections of first rate essays); *The Comedy of Manners*, by John Palmer; *Comedy and Conscience After the Restoration*, by J. W. Krutch; *Playgoer's Handbook to Restoration Drama*, by Malcolm Elwin; *The Commonwealth and Restoration Stage*, by Leslie Hotson; *The Restoration Comedy of Wit*, by T. H. Fujimura; *The First Modern Comedies*, by N. H. Holland (a fresh approach to Restoration comedy); *History of Eighteenth Century Drama*, by Allardyce Nicoll; *Shakespeare to Sheridan*, by Alwin Thaler; *The Drama of Sensibility*, by Ernest Bernbaum; *English Comic Drama, 1700–1750*, by F. W. Bateson; *History of Early Nineteenth Century Drama* and *History of Late Nineteenth Century Drama*, by Allardyce Nicoll; *Sheridan to Robertson*, by E. B. Watson; *History of Modern Drama*, by Barrett Clark and George Freedley; *Modern Drama*, by Martin Lamm; *Drama from Ibsen to Eliot*, by Raymond Williams; *His-*

tory of the American Drama, by A. H. Quinn; *Fifty Years of American Drama,* by Alan Downer; *On the Art of the Theater* and *The Theater Advancing,* by Kenneth Macgowan; *An Outline of Contemporary Drama,* by T. H. Dickinson; *Aspects of Modern Drama,* by F. W. Chandler; *A Study of the Modern Drama,* by Barrett Clark; and *The American Drama since 1918,* by J. W. Krutch.

The texts of plays from all periods of dramatic history are easily obtainable today, especially in the many paperback series and editions. *The Complete Greek Drama,* edited by W. J. Oates and Eugene O'Neill, Jr., and *Complete Roman Plays,* edited by G. E. Duckworth, are good collections; there are many shorter anthologies and translations of individual plays. Anthologies containing early English, pre-Elizabethan, Elizabethan, and Jacobean plays are *English Miracle Plays, Moralities, and Interludes,* by A. W. Pollard; *Chief Pre-Shakespearean Dramas,* by J. Q. Adams; *English Drama 1580–1642,* by C. F. T. Brooke and N. B. Paradise; and *Elizabethan and Jacobean Plays,* by Baskerville, Heltzel, and Nethercot. Shakespeare's plays are available in many editions; the New Cambridge and Arden series are excellent editions of the individual plays; *Complete Plays and Poems of Shakespeare,* by W. H. Neilson and C. J. Hill, is a good collection. Elizabethan and later plays may be found in the well known "Mermaid" and "Belles Lettres" series. A well edited and representative collection is *Plays of the Restoration and Eighteenth Century,* by Dougald MacMillan and H. M. Jones. T. H. Dickinson has edited three series of *Chief Contemporary Dramatists. A Treasury of the Theatre,* latest edition, edited by John Gassner, contains seventy-one plays from Aeschylus to Ionesco in two volumes. *Twenty-Five Modern Plays,* third edition, by S. M. Tucker and Alan Downer; and *Contemporary Drama,* by E. B. Watson and Benfield Pressey, are excellent collections. Collections of American plays are *Representative American Plays,* seventh edition, by A. H. Quinn; and the five volume Library of *Best American Plays,* edited by John Gassner; which contains ninety-six plays covering the years 1916 to 1957. Valuable for statistical purposes and also for abbreviated texts of the plays they contain, are the annual *Best Plays,* now edited by John Chapman, which began with the year 1919–1920; together with the volume *Best Plays of 1909–1919,* they provide a running commentary of the American Theater from 1909 to the present.

INDEX